CAMBRIDGE PRIMARY
Mathematics

Games Book

Cherri Moseley and Janet Rees

CAMBRIDGE
UNIVERSITY PRESS

University Printing House, Cambridge CB2 8BS, United Kingdom

One Liberty Plaza, 20th Floor, New York, NY 10006, USA

477 Williamstown Road, Port Melbourne, VIC 3207, Australia

314–321, 3rd Floor, Plot 3, Splendor Forum, Jasola District Centre,
New Delhi – 110025, India

79 Anson Road, #06–04/06, Singapore 079906

Cambridge University Press is part of the University of Cambridge.

It furthers the University's mission by disseminating knowledge in the pursuit of
education, learning and research at the highest international levels of excellence.

Information on this title: education.cambridge.org

© Cambridge University Press 2014

First published 2014

20 19 18 17 16 15 14 13

Printed in Italy by Rotolito S.p.A.

A catalogue record for this publication is available from the British Library

ISBN 978-1-107-62349-1 Paperback

Cover artwork: Bill Bolton

Cambridge University Press has no responsibility for the persistence or accuracy
of URLs for external or third-party internet websites referred to in this publication,
and does not guarantee that any content on such websites is, or will remain,
accurate or appropriate.

NOTICE TO TEACHERS IN THE UK
It is illegal to reproduce any part of his work in material form (including photocopying
and electronic storage) except under the following circumstances:

(i)   where you are abiding by a licence granted to your school or institution by the
       Copyright Licensing Agency;
(ii)   where no such licence exists, or where you wish to exceed the terms of a licence, and
       you have gained the written permission of Cambridge University Press;
(iii) where you are allowed to reproduce without permission under the provisions
       of Chapter 3 of the Copyright, Designs and Patents Act 1988, which covers, for
       example, the reproduction for the purposes of setting examination questions.

NOTICE TO TEACHERS
The photocopy masters in this publication may be photocopied or distributed
[electronically] free of charge for classroom use within the school or institution that
purchased the publication. Worksheets and copies of them remain in the copyright
of Cambridge University Press, and such copies may not be distributed or used in
any way outside the purchasing institution.

CD-ROM Terms and conditions of use

This End User License Agreement ('EULA') is a legal agreement between 'You' (which means the individual customer)
and Cambridge University Press ('the Licensor') for *Cambridge Primary Mathematics Games Book Stage 2* CD-ROM
('the Product'). Please read this EULA carefully. By continuing to use the Product, You agree to the terms of this
EULA. If You do not agree to this EULA, please do not use this Product and promptly return it to the place where you
obtained it.

1. Licence
The Licensor grants You the right to use the Product under the terms of this EULA as follows:
(a) You may only install one copy of this Product (i) on a single computer or secure network server for use by one or
    more people at different times, or (ii) on one or more computers for use by a single person (provided the Product is
    only used on one computer at one time and is only used by that single person).
(b) You may only use the Product for non-profit, educational purposes.
(c) You shall not and shall not permit anyone else to: (i) copy or authorise copying of the Product, (ii) translate the
    Product, (iii) reverse-engineer, disassemble or decompile the Product, or (iv) transfer, sell, assign or otherwise
    convey any portion of the Product.

2. Copyright
(a) All content provided as part of the Product (including text, images and ancillary material) and all software, code,
    and metadata related to the Product is the copyright of the Licensor or has been licensed to the Licensor, and is
    protected by copyright and all other applicable intellectual property laws and international treaties.
(b) You may not copy the Product except for making one copy of the Product solely for backup or archival purposes.
    You may not alter, remove or destroy any copyright notice or other material placed on or with this Product.
(c) You may edit and make changes to any material provided in the Product in editable format ('Editable Material')
    and store copies of the resulting files ('Edited Files') for your own non-commercial, educational use, but You may
    not distribute Editable Materials or Edited Files to any third-party, or remove, alter, or destroy any copyright
    notices on Editable Materials or Edited Files, or copy any part of any Editable Material or Edited Files into any
    other file for any purpose whatsoever.

3. Liability and Indemnification
(a) The Product is supplied 'as-is' with no express guarantee as to its suitability. To the extent permitted by applicable
    law, the Licensor is not liable for costs of procurement of substitute products, damages or losses of any kind
    whatsoever resulting from the use of this Product, or errors or faults therein, and in every case the Licensor's
    liability shall be limited to the suggested list price or the amount actually paid by You for the Product, whichever is
    lower.
(b) You accept that the Licensor is not responsible for the persistency, accuracy or availability of any URLs of external
    or third-party internet websites referred to on the Product and does not guarantee that any content on such
    websites is, or will remain, accurate, appropriate or available. The Licensor shall not be liable for any content made
    available from any websites and URLs outside the Product or for the data collection or business practices of any
    third-party internet website or URL referenced by the Product.
(c) You agree to indemnify the Licensor and to keep indemnified the Licensor from and against any loss, cost, damage
    or expense (including without limitation damages paid to a third party and any reasonable legal costs) incurred by
    the Licensor as a result of your breach of any of the terms of this EULA.

4. Termination
Without prejudice to any other rights, the Licensor may terminate this EULA if You fail to comply with any of its
terms and conditions. In such event, You must destroy all copies of the Product in your possession.

5. Governing law
This agreement is governed by the laws of England and Wales, without regard to its conflict of laws provision, and
each party irrevocably submits to the exclusive jurisdiction of the English courts. The parties disclaim the application
of the United Nations Convention on the International Sale of Goods.

Contents

Number

100 square muddle	1
100 square games (1 and 2)	3
100 target (1 to 3)	5
Playing with 20 (1 to 4)	7
Adding game	10
Multiplication grid	12
Playing with 100 (1 to 3)	14
Place value games (1 and 2)	17
To 100 and back again!	17
Collect 20	22
Doubles game	22
Make 100	25
10 difference	25
2, 5, 10 game	27
Remainders game	27
Dice doubles or Spinner doubles	31
3 and 4 race	31
10 plus 10 minus Game	36
Peek a boo!	38
Fraction game	40
3s and 4s game	40
Four remainders	43
Greater than/Less than game	43

Measure

Snakes and ladders	47
Rally track	51
Sports day (1 and 2)	54
The baking game (1 and 2)	58
Slide, slip and spill	62
Hare and tortoise (1 and 2)	65
Time travel (1 and 2)	67

Geometry

Shape match (1–4)	70
Name that shape	74
Collect and build shapes (1 and 2)	76
The symmetry game (1 and 2)	78
Where is it?	79

Handling data

Track the Trolls (1 and 2)	83

Introduction

This Games Book consolidates and reinforces mathematical learning for Stage2 learners (usually 6–7 years). It can be used as an independent resource for anyone wanting to encourage mathematical learning in children, or as a supplementary part of the *Cambridge Primary Mathematics* series.

If used as part of the series alongside the *Teacher's Resource 2* (9781107640733), then you will often be going directly to a specific game and page number according to the reference in the '*More activities*' section in the *Teacher's Resource* and will therefore already be familiar with the learning outcome of the game. If you are using the book as an independent resource, you can use the Objective map on the CD-ROM to help you determine what game you might want to play according to what learning outcome you are after, or you can simply read the '*Maths focus*' at the start of each game to decide if it's appropriate.

The games are grouped by strand, i.e. 'Number', 'Geometry', 'Measure' and 'Handling data' so that an independent user can easily navigate the pool of games. For those of you using this book alongside the *Teacher's Resource 5*, you will find that the games within a strand are ordered according to the order in which they are referenced in the *Teacher's Resource 2* (if you grouped all chapters of a given strand together).

Please note that the *Games Book* on its own does **not** cover all of the Cambridge Primary mathematics curriculum framework for Stage 2.

All games boards, game cards and record sheets provided within the printed book are also available on the CD-ROM for quick printing if preferred. Some games boards and resources will also be provided as Word documents so that you can adapt them as required. The CD-ROM also provides child-friendly instructions for each game, which can be displayed at the front of the class or sent home with the games for independent play. Nets for making dice, spinners and other useful mathematical resources are also provided as printable PDFs on the CD-ROM.

 This publication is part of the *Cambridge Primary Maths* project. *Cambridge Primary Maths* is an innovative combination of curriculum and resources designed to support teachers and learners to succeed in primary mathematics through best-practice international maths teaching and a problem-solving approach.

Cambridge Primary Maths brings together the world-class Cambridge Primary mathematics curriculum from Cambridge International Examinations, high-quality publishing from Cambridge University Press and expertise in engaging online enrichment materials for the mathematics curriculum from NRICH.

Teachers have access to an online tool that maps resources and links to materials offered through the primary mathematics curriculum, NRICH and Cambridge Primary mathematics textbooks and e-books. These resources include engaging online activities, best-practice guidance and examples of *Cambridge Primary Maths* in action.

The Cambridge curriculum is dedicated to helping schools develop learners who are confident, responsible, reflective, innovative and engaged. It is designed to give learners the skills to problem solve effectively, apply mathematical knowledge and develop a holistic understanding of the subject.

The *Cambridge Primary Maths* textbooks provide best-in-class support for this problem-solving approach, based on pedagogical practice found in successful schools across the world. The engaging NRICH online resources help develop mathematical thinking and problem-solving skills. To get involved visit www.cie.org.uk/cambridgeprimarymaths

The benefits of being part of *Cambridge Primary Maths* are:
- the opportunity to explore a maths curriculum founded on the values of the University of Cambridge and best practice in schools
- access to an innovative package of online and print resources that can help bring the Cambridge Primary mathematics curriculum to life in the classroom.

This series is arranged to ensure that the curriculum is covered whilst allowing teachers to use a flexible approach. The Scheme of Work for Stage 2 has been followed, though not in the same order and there will be some deviations. The components are:
- Teacher's Resource 2 ISBN: 9781107640733 (printed book and CD-ROM).
- Learner's Book 2 ISBN: 9781107615823 (printed book)
- Games Book 2 ISBN: 9781107623491 (printed book and CD-ROM).

For associated NRICH activities, please visit the *Cambridge Primary Maths* project at www.cie.org.uk/cambridgeprimarymaths

100 square muddle

Maths focus: becoming familiar with the layout and patterns of numbers in a 100 square.

A game for two or three players

You will need:
- Game board (page 2).
- A different coloured counter (or alternative) for each player.
- A 1–6 dice (CD-ROM).

How to play

1. In order to help players work out where to move their counter to, it may be useful to explore which numbers have been swapped and how they link to each other before starting the game.

2. Players put their coloured counter on start (1) then take it in turns to roll the dice and move their counter along the 100 square by the number of spaces shown on the dice. Players need to take care to progress along the square, and at the end of each row, they must move their counter on to the beginning of the next row.

3. Some of the numbers have been swapped. If a player lands on a swapped number (for example 60 in the first row) they must move their counter to where the correct number is (in this case, 6). Sometimes this will take them closer to the Finish (100) and sometimes this will take them back towards the start. The winner is the first player to land on 100.

Challenge

For a more challenging game, give players a 100 square and a blank 100 square to enable them to make up their own 100 square muddle. They could play the game with a partner or challenge them to spot and colour the swaps.

10	20	30	40	50	6	70	80	90	100 Finish
9	91	29	39	94	59	69	79	98	99
8	18	28	83	48	85	68	87	88	89
7	17	27	37	74	57	76	77	78	97
60	16	26	36	46	65	66	67	86	96
5	15	52	35	54	55	56	75	58	95
4	14	24	43	44	45	64	47	84	49
3	31	23	33	34	53	63	73	38	93
2	21	22	32	42	25	62	72	82	92
1 Start	11	12	13	41	51	61	71	81	19

100 square games (1 and 2)

Maths focus: learning the number pattern produced when adding or subtracting 10 repeatedly.

A game for two or three players

You will need:
- Game board (page 4).
- A different coloured counter (or alternative) for each player.
- A 1–6 dice (CD-ROM).

Game 1: Adding 10

How to play

1. Players put their coloured counter on any single–digit number. Players then take it in turns to roll the dice. If the number rolled is odd (1, 3 or 5) the player's counter stays where it is. If the number rolled is even (2, 4 or 6) the player moves their counter one row down the 100 square, adding ten.

2. Players record their journey down the hundred square. For example if the player starts on 6:

   $6+10 = 16$

   $16+10 = 26$

   $26+10 = 36$ and so on.

3. The winner is the first player to reach the bottom row of the 100 square.

Game 2: Taking away 10

How to play

1. As Game 1, but players start by putting their coloured counter on any number in the last row of the 100 square, 91 to 100. Players then take it in turns to roll the dice. If the number rolled is odd (1, 3 or 5) the player's counter stays where it is. If the number rolled is even (2, 4 or 6) the player moves their counter one row up the 100 square, taking away (subtracting) ten. For example if the player starts on 93:

   $93-10 = 83$

   $83-10 = 73$

   $73-10 = 63$ and so on.

2. The winner is the first player to reach the first row of the 100 square.

1	2	3	4	5	6	7	8	9	10
11	12	13	14	15	16	17	18	19	20
21	22	23	24	25	26	27	28	29	30
31	32	33	34	35	36	37	38	39	40
41	42	43	44	45	46	47	48	49	50
51	52	53	54	55	56	57	58	59	60
61	62	63	64	65	66	67	68	69	70
71	72	73	74	75	76	77	78	79	80
81	82	83	84	85	86	87	88	89	90
91	92	93	94	95	96	97	98	99	100

100 target (1 to 3)

Maths focus (1 and 2): practising recognising and saying the addition and subtraction facts for the pairs of multiples of 10 with a total of 100.

A game for two players

You will need:
- Game board (page 6) for each player.
- Two sets of Game cards (CD-ROM).

How to play

Game 1: Addition

1. Players take a game board each. They shuffle the two sets of cards together and place the pile of cards face down between them.

2. The players take it in turns to turn the top card of the pile over and place it on their Game board on the the other number of the pair to make 100, saying the addition fact.
   For example, if a 60 card is turned over, the player says "60 + 40 = 100" and places the card on their 40. If the number is already covered by a card, the card is returned face down to the bottom of the pile.

3. The winner is the first player to match all the numbers on their target board.

Game 2: Subtraction

As Game 1, but the player says the subtraction fact. For example, if a 60 card is turned over, the player says "100−60 = 40" and places the card on their 40.

Game 3: Rounding

Maths focus: practising rounding numbers to the nearest 10.

A game for two players

You will need:
- Game board (page 6) for each player.
- A set of 0 to 100 number cards, with the tens numbers and zero removed (CD-ROM).

How to play

1. Players take a game board each. They shuffle the cards and place the pile of cards face down between them.

2. The players take it in turns to turn the top card over. They round the number to the nearest 10 and place the card on the appropriate tens number on their board.

3. The winner is the first player to cover all the numbers on their target board.

10	100	30	Target 100
80	50	90	20
60	0	40	70

Playing with 20 (1 to 4)

Game 1: 20 Pairs

Maths focus: recognising number pairs to 20.

Games for two players

You will need:
- Game board (page 9).
- A 1–6 dice (CD-ROM).
- (1 and 3) 20 counters (or alternative); different colour per player.
- (2 and 4) 11 to 19 counters (or alternative); depending on target number.

How to play

1. Place the 20 counters in the central oval. Each player uses one pair of Ten frames as their base board. Players take turns to roll a dice and take that number of counters from the oval. They then place one counter in each square on their base board.

2. When there are no more counters in the oval, the players have to stop and count how many counters they each have. Players should recognise that between them they have a number pair to 20. They write down the resulting number pair, for example if Player 1 has 14 counters and Player 2 has 6: $14 + 6 = 20$. The player whose turn it is next, announces what number of counters they need in order to make 20, for example Player 1 would say 'I need 6 counters'. The player then rolls the dice. If the number rolled is the number required to make 20, the player automatically wins the game. If not, they either take counters or miss a turn: if the number rolled is less than the number of counters they need, they take that many counters

from their opponent; if they roll a number that is greater than the number they need, they miss a turn. Play passes to the next player who starts by writing the new number pair and announces how many counters they need to make 20. Play continues in this way.

3. The winner is the first player to make 20.

Game 2: Playing with 11 to 19

Maths focus: recognising number pairs for target numbers from 11 to 20.

How to play

1. Players decide together what the target number will be. They then colour in squares on the second Ten frame from the bottom up, on their side of the Game board; the coloured squares represent spaces that cannot be used. In doing so, the players create a Game board with the target number of squares on either side of the board. For example, if the players choose 18 as their target number, they each colour in the bottom two squares of their second Ten frame so that there are only 18 white squares on each side of the board.

2. Put a number of counters that matches the target number in the oval. In our example, this would be 18 counters. Players take turns to roll a dice and take that number of counters from the oval. They then place one counter in each square on their base board.

3. When there are no more counters in the oval, the players have to stop and count how many counters they each have. Players should recognise that between them they have a number pair to their target number (in this case 18). They write down the resulting number pair, for example if Player 1 has 8 counters and Player 2 has 10: $8 + 10 = 18$. The player whose turn it is next, announces what number of counters they need

in order to make the target number. The player then rolls the dice. If the number rolled is the number required to make the target number, the player automatically wins the game. If not, they either take counters or miss a turn: if the number rolled is less than the number of counters they need, they take that many counters from their opponent; if they roll a number that is greater than the number they need, they miss a turn. Play passes to the next player who starts by writing the new number pair and announces how many counters they need to make the target number. Play continues in this way.

4. The winner is the first player to reach the target number.

Game 3: 20 take away

Maths focus: recognising subtraction pairs to 20.

How to play

1. Each player starts with 20 counters on their two ten frames. They take it in turns to roll a dice and remove that number of counters from their frame, placing them on the oval. Players can only remove the number of counters that is indicated by the number on the dice. For example, if they throw a 5, but have only four counters, they miss a turn.

2. As a player removes counters from their ten frames, they record the subtraction they have carried out. So if a player starts by rolling a 3 and removes three counters, they can record this as $20 - 3 = 17$. If their next roll of the dice is a 5, they remove five more counters. Their ten frames now show $20 - 8 = 12$ as they have taken away eight counters altogether and they have 12 counters left on their ten frames.

3. The winner is the first player to have no counters left on their Ten frames.

Game 4: 11 to 19 take away

Maths focus: recognising subtraction pairs for target numbers from 11 to 20.

How to play

1. Players choose a target number and set up the Game board as per Playing with 20 (2), colouring in squares that are not to be used, and putting the appropriate number of counters on the oval.

2. As players remove counters from their ten frames, they record the subtraction they have carried out. So if the target number is 18 and a player starts by rolling a 3 and removes three counters, they can record this as $18 - 3 = 15$. If their next roll of the dice is a 5, they remove five more counters. Their ten frames now show $18 - 8 = 10$ as they have taken away eight counters altogether and as they have ten counters left on their ten frame.

3. The winner is the first player to have no counters left on their Ten frames.

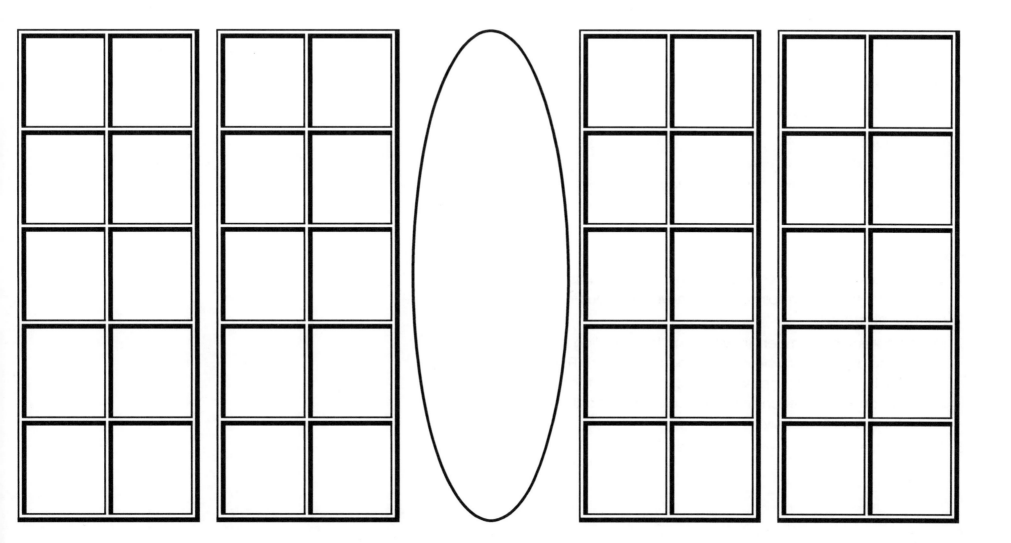

Adding game

Maths focus: practising addition strategies.

A game for two players

You will need:
- Game board (page 11).
- A counter (or alternative) for each player.
- A 1–6 dice or spinner (CD-ROM).

How to play

1. Players place their counter on Start. They take it in turns to roll the dice (or to spin the spinner) and move their counter that number of spaces.

2. Players collect the numbers they land on by recording them on a piece of paper or whiteboard. When they reach Finish, they total their numbers any way they choose. They then swap lists and check each other's calculation by adding the numbers in a different way.

3. The winner is the player with the greatest total.

Adding game – Game board

Multiplication grid

Maths focus: practising multiplication.

A game for two players

You will need:
- Game board (page 13).
- 1–6 dice (CD-ROM).
- 2, 5, 10, dice (CD-ROM).
- Counters (or alternative) in two different colours.

How to play

1. Players take it in turns to roll both the 1–6 dice and the 2, 5, 10 dice. The 1 to 6 tells them 'how many times' and the 2, 5, 10 tells them the number they are multiplying. So a '3' scored on the 1–6 dice and a '10' scored on the 2, 5, 10 dice means 3 times 10.

2. Players multiply their dice scores together to get a new number. They place a counter on this number on the Game board. If the number is already covered, they miss that turn.

3. The winner is the first player to get three counters in a row – horizontally, vertically or diagonally.

X	1	2	3	4	5	6
2	2	4	6	8	10	12
5	5	10	15	20	25	30
10	10	20	30	40	50	60

Playing with 100 (1 to 3)

Maths focus: finding pairs of multiples of 10 with a total of 100.

Game 1: Playing with 100

A game for two players

You will need:
- Game board (page 16).
- Ten counters (or alternative), all with 10 written on the front and back (the colour of the counter is not important, but it is better if they are all the same colour).
- A 1–6 dice (CD-ROM).

How to play

1. Place the ten counters in the central oval. Players count in tens as they place each counter in the oval, to remind themselves that each counter is worth 10. Each player uses one Ten frame as their base board. Players take turns to roll a dice and take that number of counters from the oval and place one in each square on their base board.

2. When there are no more counters in the oval, the players have to stop and count how many counters they each have. Players should recognise that between them they have a number pair to 100. They write down the resulting number pair, for example if Player 1 has 4 counters and Player 2 has 6: 40 + 60 = 100. The player whose turn it is next, announces what number of counters they need in order to make 100, for example Player 1 would say 'I need 60 to make 100 so I need 6 counters'. The player then rolls the dice. If the number rolled is the number of counters required to make 100, the player automatically wins

the game. If not, they either take counters or miss a turn: if the number rolled is less than the number of counters they need, they take that many counters from their opponent; if they roll a number that is greater than the number they need, they miss a turn. Play passes to the next player who starts by writing the new number pair to 100 and announces how many counters they need to make 100. Play continues in this way.

3. The winner is the first player to make 100.

Game 2: 100 take away

A game for two players

You will need:
- Game board (page 16).
- 20 counters (or alternative), all with 10 written on the front and back (the colour of the counter is not important, but it is better if each player has a different colour).
- A 1–6 dice (CD-ROM).

How to play

1. Each player starts with ten counters on their Ten frame. They take it in turns to roll a dice and remove that number of counters from their frame, placing them on the central oval. Players can only remove the amount shown on the dice. For example, if players roll a 5 and there are only 4 counters remaining on their Ten frame, they must miss that turn because they cannot remove the number shown on the dice.

2. As players remove counters from their Ten frame, they record the subtraction they have carried out. So if a player rolls a 3 and removes three counters (worth 30), they can record this as 100 − 30 = 70. If their next roll of the dice is a 5, they remove 5 more counters (worth 50), their 10 frame is now showing

100 − 80 = 20 as they have taken away eight counters, worth and they have 2 counters, worth 20, left on their 10 frame.

3. The first player to remove all of their counters is the winner.

Game 3: Playing with 100 add and subtract

A game for two players

You will need:
- Game board (page 16).
- Ten counters (or alternative), all with 10 written on the front and back (the colour of the counter is not important, but it is better if they are all the same colour).
- A 1–6 dice (CD-ROM).

How to play
Play as per Game 1 except that the players have to write both the addition and subtraction facts for the number pair to 100. In other words, they have to write the fact family for the number pair to 100. If we use the same example as in Game 1, then when there are no more counters in the central oval the players should recognise that between them they have the counters to represent the number pair to 100 of 60 and 40. So they would write down the following fact family:

60 + 40 = 100
40 + 60 = 100
100 − 60 = 40
100 − 40 = 60.

Play then passes to the other player and continues as per Game 1.

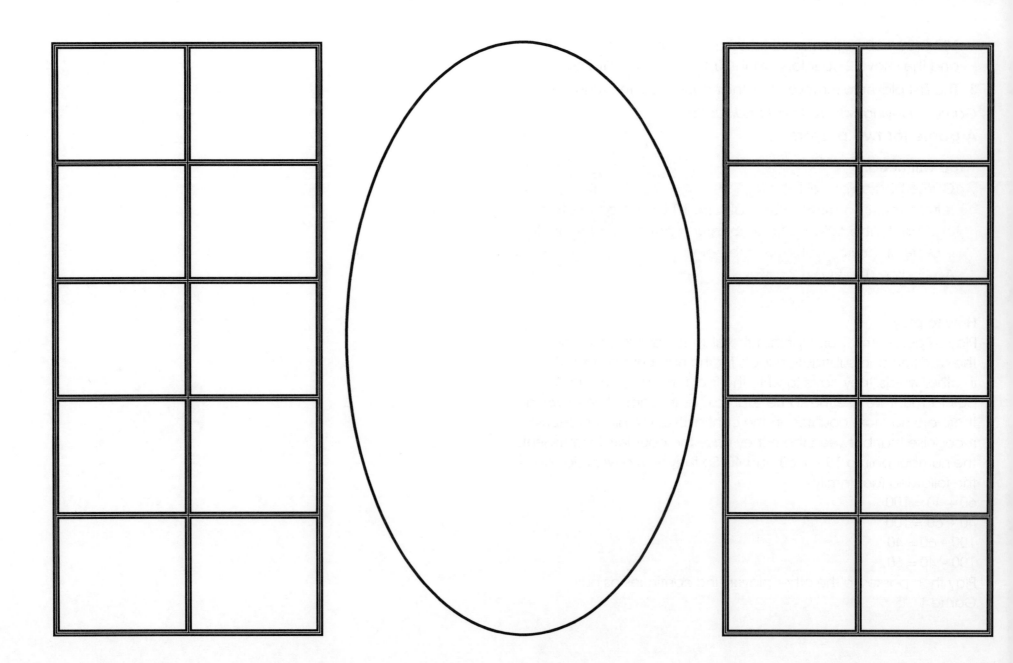

Place value games (1 and 2)

Maths focus: ordering and comparing numbers using place value.

A game for two or three players

You will need:
- Game board (page 18).
- A counter (or alternative).
- A 'Player card' for each player (page 19).
- A 1–6 dice (CD-ROM).
- Two or three sets of Place value cards (CD-ROM).
- (2) A set of 'Less than/greater than' cards.

Game 1
How to play

1. Players place their counter on 'Start'. They take turns to roll the dice and move their counter that number of spaces. Players collect the Place value card matching the numbers they land on. Players cannot collect more than one copy of each card, so if they land on a space of a card they already have, they do not collect a card.

2. When they reach 'Finish', they use their place value cards to make the numbers requested by the Player cards. Players score a point if their number is the closest or highest.

3. The winner is the player with the most points.

Challenge
For a more challenging game, each collected place value card can only be used once when making numbers to compare.

Game 2
How to play
As *Game 1* until players reach 'Finish'. They then use their cards to create number sentences using the Less than/greater than cards. The winner (or winners) is the player who uses all their cards in correct number sentences.

To 100 and back again!

Maths focus: counting forward and back in twos, fives and tens.
A game for two to four players

You will need:
- Game board (page 18).
- A counter for each player.
- A 1–6 dice (CD-ROM).
- A 100 square (CD-ROM).

How to play

1. Players place their counter on 'Start'. They take it in turns to roll the dice and move their counter that number of spaces. When the player lands on an instruction square, they must count aloud as instructed. If they are successful, they move on one space. If not, they stay where they are. Some children may like to use a 100 square for support.

2. The winner is the first player to land on 'Finish'.

Start			
1		90	100	200
2		80		300
3		70		400
4		60		500
5		50		600
6		40		700
7		30		800
8	9	20		900
		10		1	2	3

Game board squares (as laid out):

Start
1, 2, 3, 4, 5, 6, 7, 8, 9, 10
90, 80, 70, 60, 50, 40, 30, 20
100
200, 300, 400, 500, 600, 700, 800, 900
1, 2, 3
20, 30, 40
10, 9, 8, 7, 6, 5, 4
50, 60, 70, 80, 90, 100, 200
Finish

Arrow tiles:
- 7 (white) / 3 (grey)
- 7 (grey)
- 1 (light grey) / 2 (grey) / 4 (white)

Place value games (1 and 2) – Player cards

Place value game Player 1:	
Rule	Point
Closest to 45	
Closest to 100	
Closest to 200	
Smallest odd number	
Largest odd number	
Smallest even number	
Largest even number	

Place value game Player 1:	
Rule	Point
Closest to 45	
Closest to 100	
Closest to 200	
Smallest odd number	
Largest odd number	
Smallest even number	
Largest even number	

Place value game Player 1:	
Rule	Point
Closest to 45	
Closest to 100	
Closest to 200	
Smallest odd number	
Largest odd number	
Smallest even number	
Largest even number	

Place value games – Less than/greater than cards

< is less than	< is less than	> is more than	> is more than
< is less than	< is less than	> is more than	> is more than
< is less than	< is less than	> is more than	> is more than
< is less than	< is less than	> is more than	> is more than
< is less than	< is less than	> is more than	> is more than

START			Count back from 100 to 0 in tens		Count from 10 to 100 in tens			Count from 50 to 100 in fives		Count back from 20 to 0 in twos	
											Count back from 20 to 0 in fives
FINISH			Count from 80 to 100 in twos		Count from 0 to 100 in fives						Count back from 70 to 100 in twos
Count back from 20 to 0 in twos		Count back from 100 to 0 in tens			Count back from 40 to 0 in twos		Count from 40 to 100 in tens		Count from 0 to 100 in fives		Count back from 50 to 0 in tens
Count from 0 to 100 in tens											Count back from 30 to 0 in twos
		Count from 50 to 100 in fives							Count back from 70 to 0 in tens		
	Count from 0 to 100 in fives									Count from 0 to 100 in tens	

Collect 20

Maths focus: recognising the number pairs for 20.

A game for two to four players

You will need:
- Game board (page 23).
- A counter (or alternative) for each player.
- A pot of about 100 counters.
- A 1–6 dice (CD-ROM).
- Two or three sets of 0 to 20 number cards (CD-ROM).

How to play

1. Players place their counter on 'Start'. They take it in turns to roll the dice and move their counter that number of spaces.

2. Players collect the number card matching the numbers they land on, but cannot collect duplicate cards (apart from 20).

3. When they reach 'Finish', they sort out their cards into number pairs for 20:
   - If they have a number pair but no 20 to go with it, they earn one counter.
   - If they have a number pair complete with a 20, they earn two counters.

4. The player with the most counters is the winner.

Doubles game

Maths focus: identifying, practising, doubling and halving numbers.

A game for two to four players

You will need:
- Game board (page 23).
- A counter (or alternative) for each player.
- A 1–6 dice (CD-ROM).

How to play

1. Players place their counter on 'Start'. They take it in turns to roll a dice and move their counter that number of spaces.

2. If they land on a star they must double the number shown on the star; if they are not able to, they miss a turn.

3. If they land on a ribbon,

they must say what number was doubled in order to make the number on the ribbon (in other words, half the number); if they are not able to, they miss a turn.

4. The winner is the first person to land on 'Finish'.

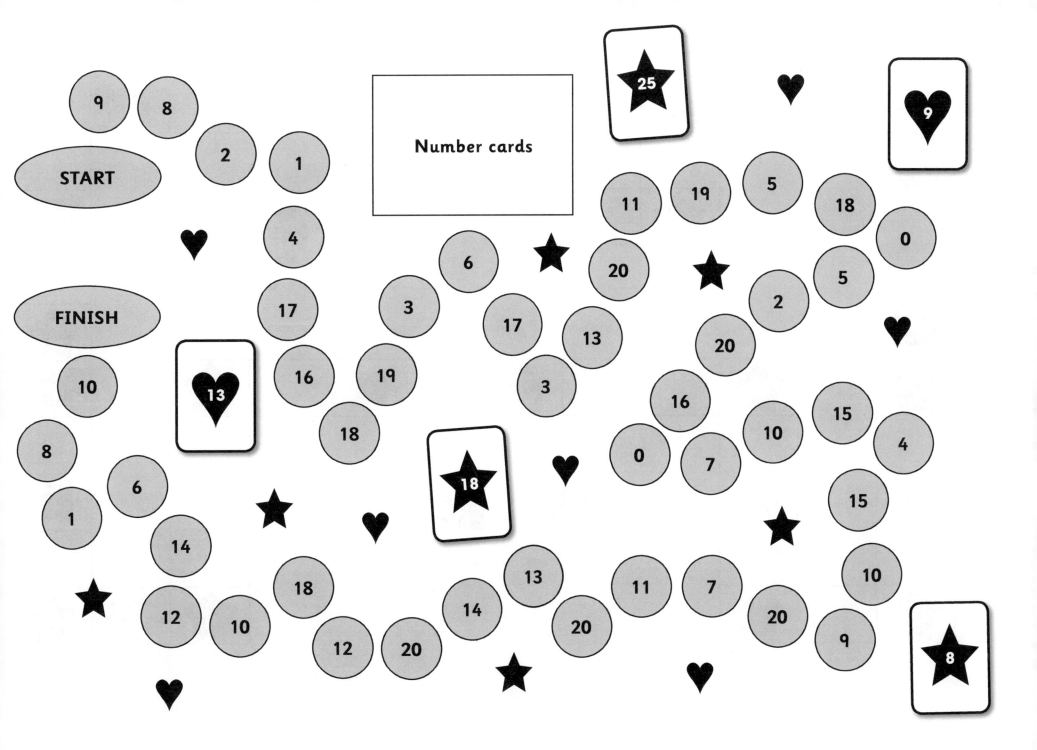

Number cards

START

FINISH

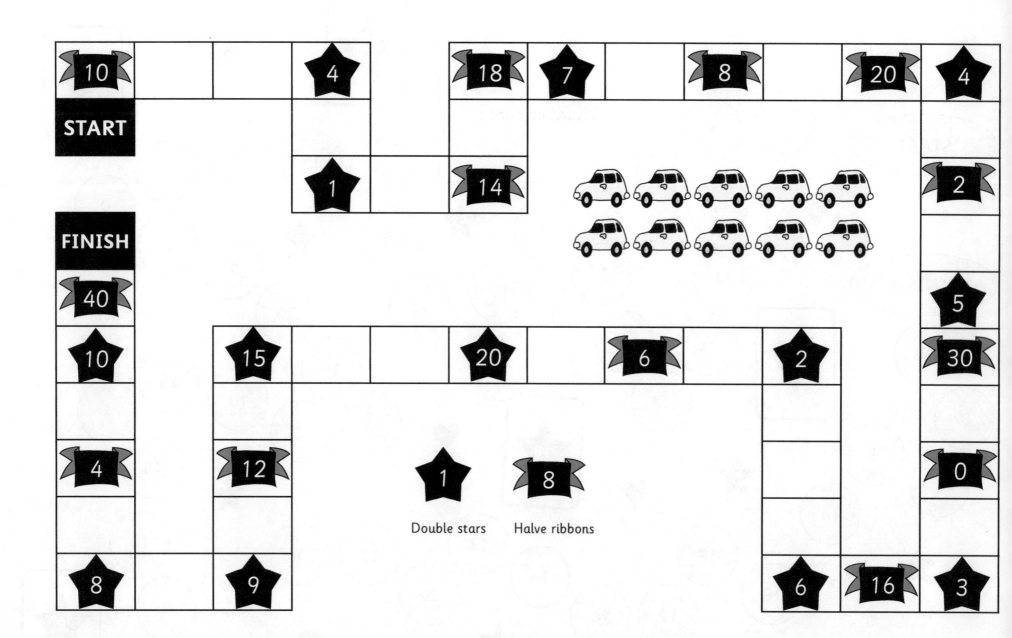

Double stars   Halve ribbons

Doubles game – Game board

Make 100

Maths focus: adding and subtracting numbers to get as close as possible to 100.

A game for two players

You will need:
- Game board (page 26).
- Two sets of 'Place value cards' (CD-ROM); use tens and ones cards only.
- A supply of counters (or alternative).

How to play

1. Players shuffle together the ones cards from both sets of Place value cards and place them face down on the table.
2. The players take it in turns to take a card from the top of the pile to place in one of the four 'ones' spaces on the game board.
3. They place the matching tens card in the tens space alongside each digit (for example: 6 in the ones space is matched with 60 in the tens space) to create a set of two-digit numbers.
4. Once all eight spaces are filled, the players add or subtract the two-digit numbers to get as close as they can to 100. Each number must be used, but can only be used once.
5. The player with the total closest to 100 wins one counter, making exactly 100 earns two counters.
6. The winner is determined at the end of at least three games, and is the player with the most counters.

10 difference

Maths focus: finding the difference, and aiming for a total difference of 10.

A game for two or three players

You will need:
- Two dice or a dice and a spinner, ideally with a different range of numbers on each.
- Paper and pencil for each player.
- A supply of counters (or alternative).

How to play

1. Players take it in turns to roll (or roll and spin) both dice.
2. On their turn, the player finds the difference between the two numbers displayed.
3. They make a note of that difference then decide whether to have one or two more turns. They are aiming to collect a difference total of 10.
4. At the end of a turn, the player adds their two or three differences together.
5. At the end of each round, when each player has taken their turn, the players compare their total difference, and score counters as follows:
   - Players with a total difference of 10 receive three counters.
   - Players with a difference of nine receive two counters.
   - Players with a difference of 11 receive one counter.
   - All other differences do not receive a counter.
6. The winner is the player with the most counters after three rounds.

tens

ones

2, 5, 10 game

Maths focus: counting in twos fives and tens.

A game for two to four players

You will need:
- Game board (page 28).
- A counter for each player.
- A 1–6 dice (CD-ROM).
- Sheet of '2, 5 and 10 stamps' (page 29).

Optional:
- Place value cards (CD-ROM)

How to play

1. Cut out the 2, 5 and 10 stamps.
2. Players place their counters on 'START'.
3. Players roll the dice and take it in turns to move their counter around the game board.
4. Each time they land on a square, they collect a matching stamp; each player creates three piles of stamps as they proceed, one pile per stamp value.
5. Once everyone has landed on 'FINISH', they count the total of each of their stamp piles; counting in twos, fives and tens as appropriate, to work out their three totals. They then add those three numbers together to find their final total.
6. The winner is the player with the highest total.

Players could use a set of place value cards to help them find their total.

Remainders game

Maths focus: creating a division calculation with a particular remainder.

A game for two to four players

You will need:
- One 'Remainders grid' for each player (page 30).
- A 1–6 dice (CD-ROM).
- Counters (or alternative).

How to play

1. Players write their name on their Remainder grid.
2. They take it in turns to roll the dice.
3. Players use the counters to help them create a division number sentence with the remainder shown on the dice. For example: if the dice shows 2, the player could get 12 counters and put them into groups of five, so two are left over. Their division sentence would be $12 \div 5 = 2 \, r2$.
4. Players tick off the remainder they have made, on their Remainder card.
5. The winner is the first player to tick off all the remainders.

START
2
5
10
2
5
10

2	5	10

2	5	10
10		2
5		5
2		10

		2	5	10
		10		2
		5		5
		2		10
		10		FINISH
2	5	10		5
				2
		2	5	10

2, 5, 10 game – Stamps

2	2	2	2	2	2	2	2	2	2
2	2	2	2	2	2	2	2	2	2
2	2	2	2	2	2	2	2	2	2
5	5	5	5	5	5	5	5	5	5
5	5	5	5	5	5	5	5	5	5
5	5	5	5	5	5	5	5	5	5
10	10	10	10	10	10	10	10	10	10
10	10	10	10	10	10	10	10	10	10
10	10	10	10	10	10	10	10	10	10

Remainders game – Remainders grid

Name		Name		Name		Name	
1		1		1		1	
2		2		2		2	
3		3		3		3	
4		4		4		4	
5		5		5		5	
6		6		6		6	

Dice doubles or Spinner doubles

Maths focus: doubling numbers 1–6.

A game for two players

You will need:

Dice game
- Game board (page 32).
- 1–6 dice (CD-ROM)
- Nine counters (or alternative) for each player.

or:

Spinner game
- Game board (page 33).
- A 1–10 spinner(page 34).
- 16 counters (or alternative) for each player.

How to play

1. Players choose which of the two game boards, left or right, they will use and take it in turns to roll the dice or spin the spinner and double the number shown. They place a counter on that number. If the number already has a counter on it, they miss that turn.

2. The winner is the first player to have a counter on every number on their game board.

3 and 4 race

Maths focus: counting in threes or fours.

A game for two players

You will need:
- Game board (page 35).
- A 1–6 dice.
- A counter or playing piece for each player.

How to play

1. Each player chooses whether to be or .

2. They place their counter on the correct 'START' then take it in turns to roll the dice and move their counter. Player 3 must roll an odd number (1, 3 or 5) to move on one space. If they roll an even number, they stay where they are. Player 4 must roll an even number (2, 4 or 6) to move on a space. If the player rolls an odd number, they must stay where they are.

3. The winner is the first player to land on the correct 'FINISH'.

Player 1

2	10	8
6	4	12
8	12	4

Player 2

4	12	2
8	2	10
6	10	6

Player 1

20	6	2	10
14	18	12	16
12	2	8	10
6	14	18	4

Player 2

4	20	14	2
16	4	10	8
8	20	6	12
10	12	16	18

1–10 spinner

To make spinner: Print out on thin card or cut out and glue on to card. Put the tip of a pencil and a paperclip on the centre. Flick the paperclip. The section with most of the paperclip in is the number to use.

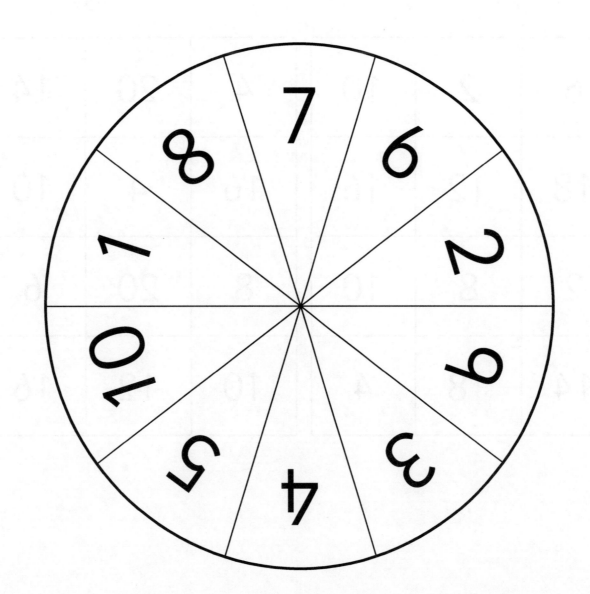

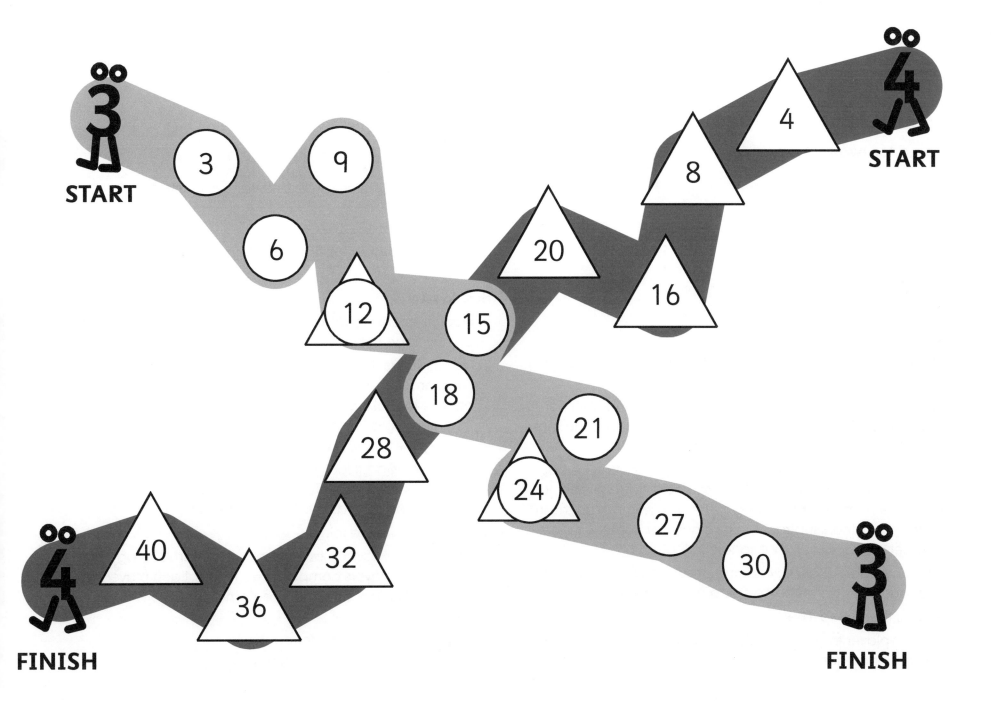

3 and 4 race – Game board

10 plus 10 minus Game

Game 1

Maths focus: adding and subtracting tens numbers from a two-digit number.

A game for two players

You will need:
- A 100 square (page 37).
- A set of 'Place value cards' (CD–ROM); use the tens cards only.
- Two 1–6 dice (CD–ROM).
- Pen.

How to play

1. Place the tens cards randomly face down on the table (or in an envelope or bag).
2. Player 1 rolls the two dice to create a two-digit number. For example, so if 4 and 2 are shown, they could choose to make 24 or 42.
3. Player 2 turns over a tens card (or takes one out of the bag or envelope without looking). Player 1 adds that number to their dice number and colours in the new number on the 100 square. They then subtract the tens number from their dice number and colour in that square in too.
4. If a number produced by adding or subtracting is not on the 100 square, it cannot be coloured and is ignored.
5. Players then swap roles.
6. The first player to get four coloured squares in any row (not column or diagonal) is the winner.

Game 2

Maths focus: adding and subtracting numbers from a three-digit number.

A game for two players

You will need:
- Win list (page 37).
- A set of 'Place value cards' (CD–ROM); use the tens cards only.
- Three 1–6 dice (CD–ROM).
- Counters (or alternative).

How to play

1. Place the tens cards randomly face down on the table (or in an envelope or bag).
2. Players 1 rolls the three dice to create a three-digit number. For example, so if 4, 5 and 2 are shown, the player could choose to make 542, 452, 245 or any other combination of the three digits rolled.
3. Player 2 turns over a tens card (or takes one out of the bag or envelope without looking). Player 1 adds that number to their dice number then subtracts the tens number from their dice number and records the result on the Win list.
4. Players then swop roles.
5. After six turns each, players check their numbers against the Win list. The players compare their results. Each player scores their result a 'win' if it more closely matches the Win list than the other player.
6. Players earn a counter for each win.
7. The winner is the player with the most counters.

100 square

1	2	3	4	5	6	7	8	9	10
11	12	13	14	15	16	17	18	19	20
21	22	23	24	25	26	27	28	29	30
31	32	33	34	35	36	37	38	39	40
41	42	43	44	45	46	47	48	49	50
51	52	53	54	55	56	57	58	59	60
61	62	63	64	65	66	67	68	69	70
71	72	73	74	75	76	77	78	79	80
81	82	83	84	85	86	87	88	89	90
91	92	93	94	95	96	97	98	99	100

Win list

Win list
Closest to 100
Closest to 1000
Closest to 500
Highest odd number
Lowest odd number
Highest even number
Lowest even number

Peek a boo!

Maths focus: developing a strategy to solve missing number calculations.

A game for two players

You will need:
- Game board (page 49).
- Ten counters (or alternative).

How to play

1. Players count out ten counters onto the table. Player 1 places a hand over the counters and slides some off the table into their other hand. Player 2 has to work out how many counters are in Player 1's hand and complete the number sentence on the game board. Player 1 then reveals the counters in their hand and checks that Player 2 is correct. They then swap over.

2. After four turns each, the players can change the number of counters they start with. They could choose to do this for every new number sentence. They must write this number in the first box of the number sentence in the section at the bottom of the game board, before they play Peek a boo! Play then continues as before until they reach the bottom of the game board.

Remember, the empty box just tells us we don't know what the number is.
The shape of the box doesn't matter.

10 − □ = ⬡

10 − ⬡ = □

10 − ⬡ = □

10 − □ = ⬡

10 − □ = ⬡

10 − ⬡ = □

10 − ⬡ = □

10 − □ = ⬡

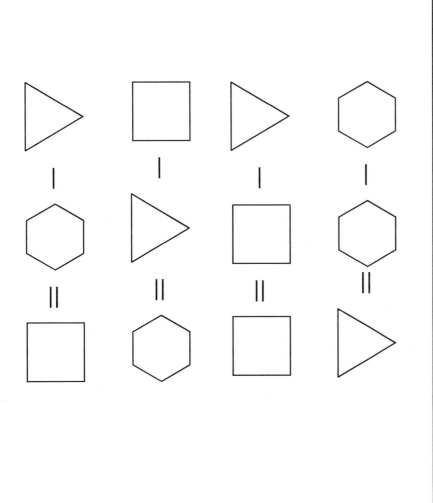

Fraction game

Maths focus: recognising which fractions ($\frac{1}{4}$, $\frac{1}{2}$ and $\frac{3}{4}$) of a square can be used to complete the square.

A game for two to four players

You will need:
- Game board for each player (page 41).
- Playing pieces for each player (page 41)
- A dice labelled $\frac{1}{4}$, $\frac{1}{2}$ and $\frac{3}{4}$. (Put a sticker over the existing numbers and write the fractions on), or use the Blank dice template on the CD-ROM).

How to play

1. Cut page 41 in two so that you separate the game board and the playing pieces. Cut out the playing pieces on the right hand side of the page. Shuffle together the different pieces and place between the players.

2. Players take it in turns to roll the dice and select the appropriate pieces:
   - If $\frac{1}{2}$ is rolled, the player may choose to take the half in two-quarters or one-half.
   - If $\frac{3}{4}$ is rolled, the player can choose either three separate quarter pieces or a half and a quarter piece.

3. Players cover their baseboard using the cut pieces as jigsaw pieces. Pieces may be arranged in whatever way the players wish but cannot be overlapped or moved once placed.

4. The winner is the first player to cover the whole of their game board.

3s and 4s game

Maths focus: counting in threes or fours.

A game for two players

You will need:
- Game board (page 42).
- A coloured counter (or alternative) for each player.
- A 1–6 dice (CD-ROM).

How to play

1. Players take it in turns to roll the dice twice. The first roll tells them how many spaces to move, the second roll tells them whether to count in threes of fours:
   - If the dice shows an odd number (1, 3 or 5) the player counts in threes.
   - If the dice shows an even number (2, 4, or 6) the player counts in fours.

2. Players then count from zero in threes or fours to the highest multiple of three or four without going past the number they landed on. Any remainder is the player's bonus score and they move on that number of spaces.

3. The first player to 50 is the winner.

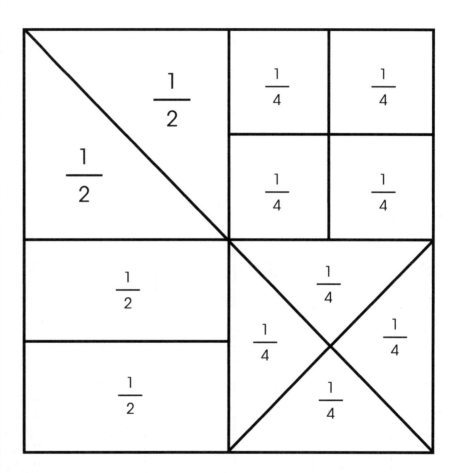

Fraction – Game board

1	2	3	4		10	11	12	13	14	15	16

START			5		9						17

			6	7	8						18

FINISH 50 — 19

49 — 20

48 | 38 | 37 | 36 | 35 | 34 | 33 | 32 | 31 — 21

47 | 39 — 30 — 22

46 | 40 — 29 — 23

45 | 41 — 28 — 24

44 | 43 | 42 — 27 | 26 | 25

3s and 4s – Game board

Four remainders

Maths focus: counting in twos, threes, fours or fives to identify a remainder.

A game for two to four players

You will need:
- Game board (page 44).
- Three 1–6 dice (CD-ROM).
- Counters (or alternative) in two different colours.

How to play

1. Players take it in turns to roll two dice and use them to create a two-digit number.
2. They then roll the third dice.
3. This time the number on the dice tells the players to count in twos, threes, fours or fives.
4. If a 1 or 6 is rolled, the player must roll again until a 2, 3, 4 or 5 is rolled.
5. Players then count from zero in twos, threes, fours or fives to the highest multiple of 2, 3, 4 or 5 without going past the number they created.
6. The remainder is their score and they place a counter on that number on the game board.
7. The winner is the first player to get four counters in a row, horizontally, vertically or diagonally.

Greater than/Less than game

Maths focus: comparing numbers using greater than and less than symbols.

A game for two players

You will need:
- Game board for each player (page 45).
- About a quarter of a set of 0 to 100 number cards (CD-ROM).
- Counters (or alternative).

How to play

1. Players decide who is Player 1 and who is Player 2 and take the appropriate base board.
2. Shuffle the number cards and put them in a pile face down between the players.
3. Players take it in turns to turn over the top card and place it on their base board, starting from the top left then top right, middle left, middle right, bottom left, bottom right.
4. After all the cards have been placed, players check each other's cards and give one counter for each correct number sentence.
5. A bonus counter is given if all three number sentences are correct.
6. Before playing the next round, players rearrange their cards to make every number sentence on their card correct if they can, to earn a further counter.
7. The player with the most counters after an agreed number of rounds is the winner.

2	**3**	**1**	**4**
4	**1**	**3**	**2**
3	**2**	**4**	**1**
1	**4**	**2**	**3**

Player 1

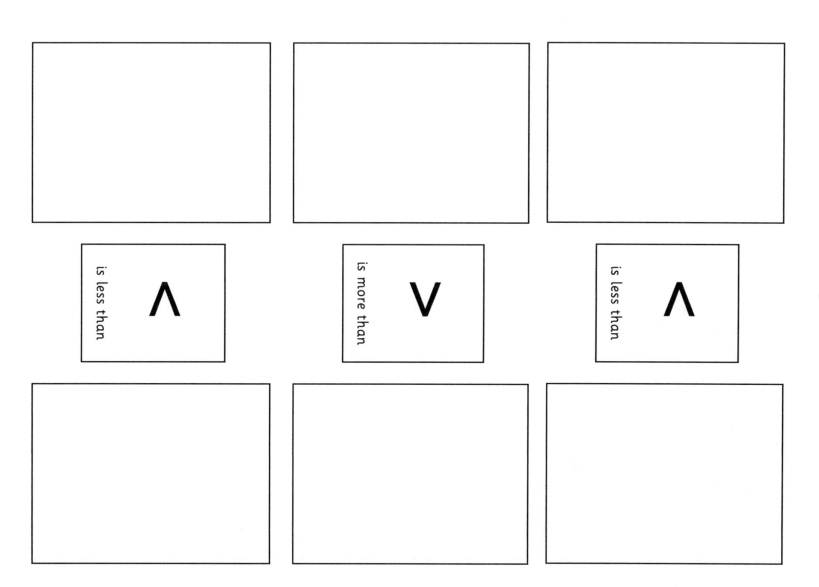

is less than
∧

is more than
∨

is less than
∧

Player 2

> is more than	< is less than	> is more than

Snakes and ladders

Maths focus: comparing lengths using direct comparison, standard units and centimetres.

A game for two to four players

You will need:
- Game board (page 48).
- A counter (or alternative) per player (marked to match the Game cards – plain, spots, stripes and zigzags).
- A set of Game cards per player (page 49).
- 1–6 dice (CD-ROM)
- Measuring equipment (rules, tape measure).

How to play

Game 1

1. Give each player a set of game cards of one type (plain, spots, stripes or zigzags) and a counter with the same pattern.
2. All players take the head of their snake and set aside the tail. The rest of the cards are placed on the table next to the players.
3. Decide who is going to go first. Roll the dice and move the counter that number of places:
   - If you land on the head of a snake, go down it to the tail.
   - If you land at the bottom of a ladder, go up it to the top.
   - If you land on a section of snake take a section card from the player who has that pattern.
4. Keep playing until one player reaches the 'FINISH', when all play stops and each player puts together **all** the snake pieces they have (regardless of pattern)..

5. The player with the longest snake is the winner.

Game 2

As *Game 1*, except if you land on a section of snake that matches your own pattern, take two section cards from your own pile.

Game 3

1. As *Game 2*, but once all play has stopped players can exchange pieces of snake with other players. The aim is to get the longest snake of their own pattern.
2. Once exchanging has finished, the person with the longest snake is the winner.

Game 4

1. Using the cards and the board or just the cards, ask players to make their own board game which can then be played with others in the class.

Teaching notes

These games show progression through the skills of playing games.
Game 1: This game uses basic comparison of length by either direct comparison or by measuring using centimetres.
Game 2: This game builds on the previous one but extends it to using more parts, thus increasing the lengths of the snakes made.
Game 3: This game uses reasoning in order to work with other players in order to get the longest snake of a single pattern.
The pictures around the edge of the board can be used as discussion starters or incorporated into a game players devise for themselves.

Snakes and ladders - Game cards

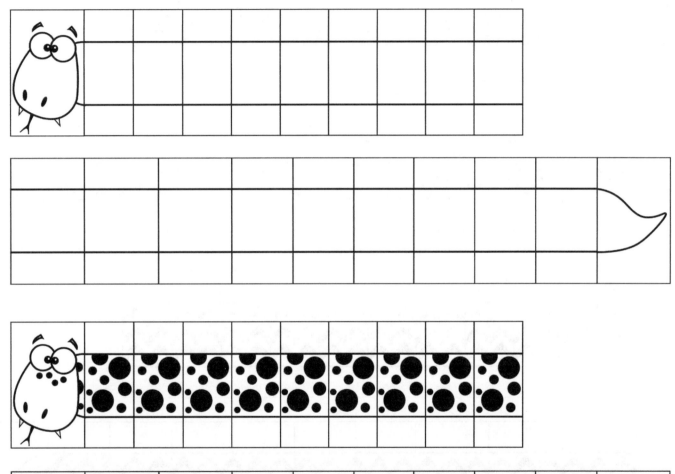

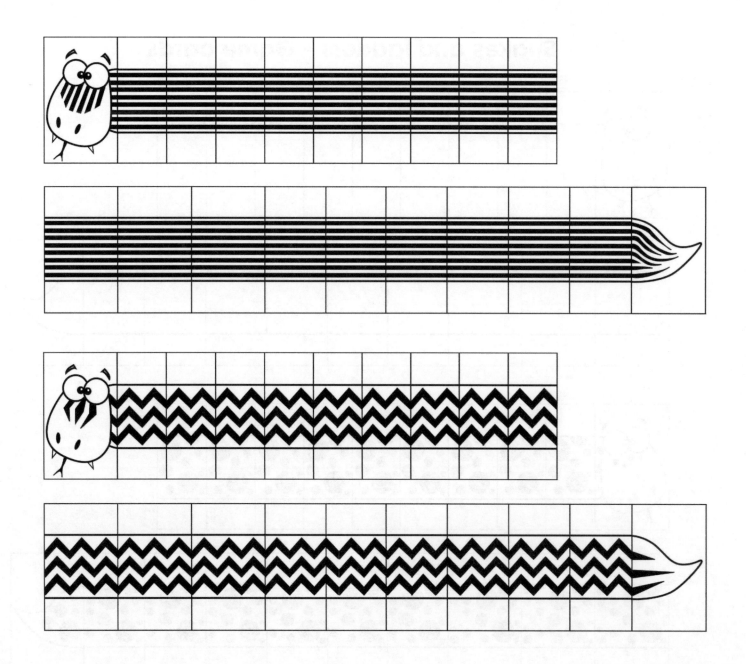

Rally track

Maths focus: using the language of measures e.g. 'shorter', 'longer'.

A game for two to four players

You will need:
- Game board (page 52).
- 1–6 dice (CD-ROM).
- A playing piece for each player (page 53).
- A set of obstacle cards (page 53).

How to play

Game 1

1. Each player chooses their car and places it on 'Start'.
2. Players take turns to roll the dice and move that number of spaces. When the road splits, players must decide which track to follow.
3. If a player lands on an obstacle, they take a matching card and follow the instructions.
4. The player who reaches the 'Finish' first is the winner.

Game 2

As *Game 1*, but if a player lands on a section numbered the same as their car, they have another go. If a player lands on a numbered section not the same as their car, they miss a turn.

Teaching notes

The aim of these games is to be the first player to get to the finish line. As play continues the players will need to make decisions about which way to go. These may or may not help them to get to the end first. There is also the element of chance created by using a dice.

At the end of the game encourage the players to talk about what they did, the results of what they did and why they changed their mind when playing the game again. Encourage the use of vocabulary such as 'longer' (distance and time), 'shorter' (distance and time), 'about the same as', (distance and time). This can be done as a whole class or with small groups.

Ask, "*Can you tell us your method? Did it work? Can you explain why it works? Did you change your mind during the game? What did you learn or find out? If you were doing it again, what would you do differently? What are the key points or ideas that you need to remember for the next time you play?*"

Encourage pairs or small groups of players to design and make their own race game with race board and playing pieces which can be played with the rest of the class.

START

FINISH

Obstacle cards

Rally track – Playing pieces

Cut out the four pieces and fold along the solid lines to make the cars stand up.

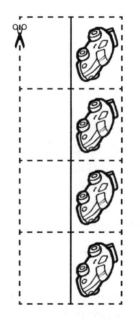

Rally track – Obstacle cards

Fallen tree: turn round and go a different way

Fallen rocks: miss 2 turns

Flock of sheep on the road: miss 2 turns OR turn around and go a different way

Go through a flood: miss a turn

Deep hole in the road: miss a turn

Collapsed bridge: miss a turn

Sports day (1 and 2)

Maths focus: using the units of length, height and time, and comparing total measurements.

A game for two, three or four players

You will need:
- Game board (page 55).
- 1–6 dice (CD-ROM).
- A counter (or alternative) for each player.
- A set of 'Measure' cards (page 56).
- Three recording grids per player (page 57).

How to play
Please note that there are three different 'sports' around the track; the success of each sport is determined by a different measure. For 'length', the sport is long jump, where the winner is the person who jumps the longest distance. For 'time' the sport is balancing, where the winner is the person who can balance for the longest time. The 'height' sport is high jump, where the winner is the person who can jump the highest.

Game 1

1. Shuffle the 'Length cards' and place them face down on the appropriate section of the board. Do the same with the 'Time' and 'Height cards'.

2. Players label one of their recording grids 'Length', one 'Height' and one 'Time', and then place their counter at 'Start' on the game board.

3. Players take turns to roll the dice and move that number of spaces along the track.

4. When a player reaches a shaded section, they take a measure card from the appropriate pile and place it on one of their recording grids.

5. Players continue to collect cards by travelling around the track, until all players' grids are full. The game can be played using 2 × 2, 3 × 3 or 4 × 4 recording grids; the larger the grid the longer the game will take to play. However, within any one game, all the grids used should be the same size.

6. Players then calculate the total for each set of their cards, one total for each grid: the total height, the total length, and the total time. Each value represents what they got for each sport.

7. The winner of each sport is the player with the highest total for that sport.

Game 2

1. As *Game 1*, but each player has only one recording grid and all players collect only cards from one sport; players agree on the sport at the start of the game. All other shaded sections on the track will be ignored.

Teaching notes
This game involves travelling along a track collecting cards with length, height or time measurements. It gives players opportunities to use their knowledge of the relationships between consecutive units of time and to add related facts for centimetres and metres.

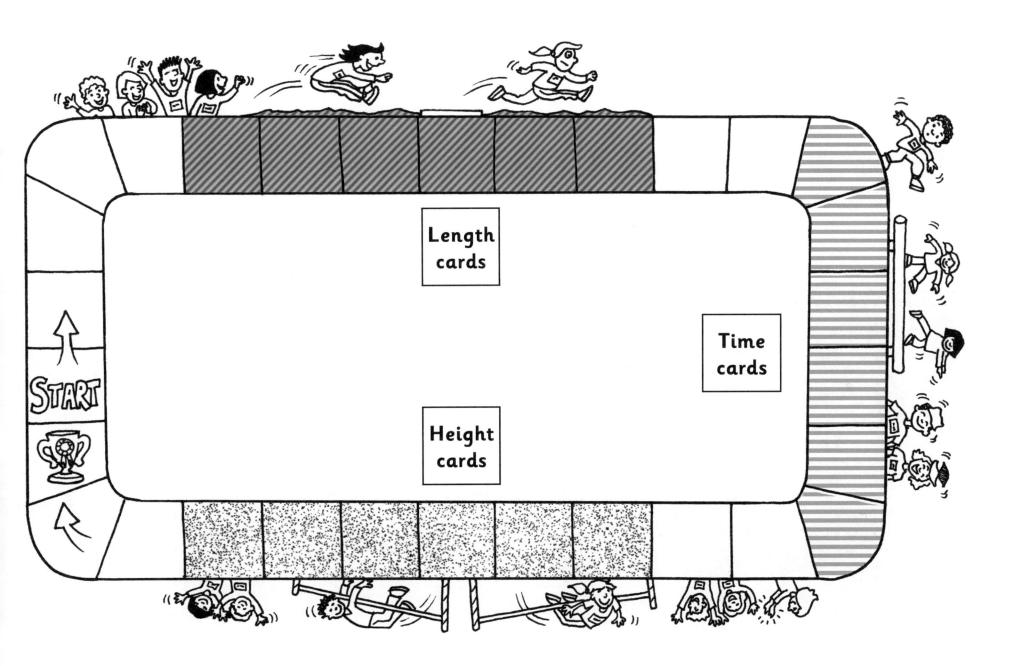

Length cards

Height cards

Time cards

START

Sports day – Measure cards

Make two copies of this page so that you have 48 'Length cards', 48 'Time cards' and 48 'Height cards'.

Length				Time				Height			
10 cm	10 cm	10 cm	10 cm	10 seconds	10 seconds	10 seconds	10 seconds	10 cm	10 cm	10 cm	10 cm
50 cm	50 cm	50 cm	50 cm	60 seconds	60 seconds	60 seconds	60 seconds	20 cm	20 cm	20 cm	20 cm
1 m	1 m	1 m	1 m	1 minute	1 minute	1 minute	1 minute	50 cm	50 cm	50 cm	50 cm
2 m	2 m	2 m	2 m	20 seconds	20 seconds	20 seconds	20 seconds	1 m	1 m	1 m	1 m
1 m 50cm	1 m 50cm	1 m 50cm	1 m 50cm	2 minutes	2 minutes	2 minutes	2 minutes	5 cm	5 cm	5 cm	5 cm
20 cm	20 cm	20 cm	20 cm	30 seconds	30 seconds	30 seconds	30 seconds	15 cm	15 cm	15 cm	15 cm

Sports day – Recording grids

Learners label their grids on the tab provided.

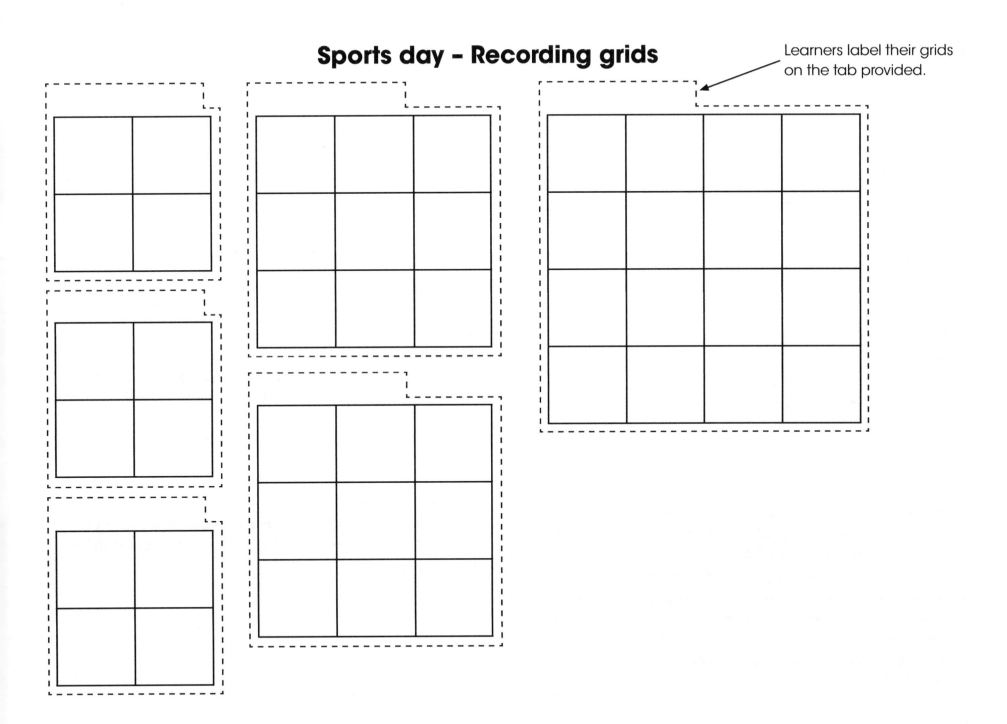

The baking game (1 and 2)

Maths focus: using the standard units of grams and exploring number problems in the context of weight.

A game for two to four players

You will need:
- Game board. (page 59)
- 1–6 dice (CD-ROM).
- Set of 'Ingredients cards' (CD-ROM).
- A 'Recipe card' per player (page 61).
- One counter (or alternative) per player.

How to play

Game 1

1. Each player places their counter on 'START'.
2. Shuffle the 'Flour' cards and place them face down on the appropriate section of the board. Do the same with the 'Sugar' and 'Margarine' cards.
3. Players take turns to roll the dice and move that number of places.
4. If a player lands on an ingredients square they take an 'Ingredients card', if they land on a square with an instruction, they must follow that instruction.
5. Play continues until every player has reached the 'FINISH'.
6. Players total the amount of each ingredient and, using their recipe card, calculate how many batches of ten biscuits they can make. For example:
200 g flour + 100 g sugar + 100 g margarine = one batch (10 biscuits).

300 g flour + 200 g sugar + 100 g margarine = one batch (10 biscuits) with 200 g flour and 100 g sugar left over.
400 g flour + 200 g sugar + 200 g, margarine = two batches (20 biscuits).

7. The player who can make the most biscuits is the winner.

Game 2

As *Game 1*, but players can also count half batches of biscuits. For example:
200 g flour + 50 g sugar + 100 g margarine = $\frac{1}{2}$ a batch (5 biscuits) with 50 g margarine and 100 g flour left over.
300 g flour + 150 g sugar + 150 g margarine = $1\frac{1}{2}$ batches (15 biscuits).

Game 2 extends knowledge and understanding from the previous game.

Challenge

1. For a more challenging game, tell players to go round the board more than once – this will mean they collect more cards to total at the end.
2. Challenge them to use the board and playing pieces to make a game of their own. They can change the recipe, change the weights and/or change the rules. This will enable you to see who has understood the main focus of the game.
3. Give prices for each of the ingredients so players are not only calculating the total weight of the biscuits but also the price.

Baking game – Ingredients cards

100 g margarine	100 g margarine	100 g margarine	100 g margarine	100 g margarine
50 g margarine	50 g margarine	50 g margarine	50 g margarine	50 g margarine
100 g sugar	100 g sugar	100 g sugar	100 g sugar	100 g sugar
50 g sugar	50 g sugar	50 g sugar	50 g sugar	50 g sugar
250 g flour	250 g flour	250 g flour	250 g flour	250 g flour
100 g flour	100 g flour	100 g flour	100 g flour	100 g flour
50 g flour	50 g flour	50 g flour	50 g flour	50 g flour

Recipe for 10 biscuits

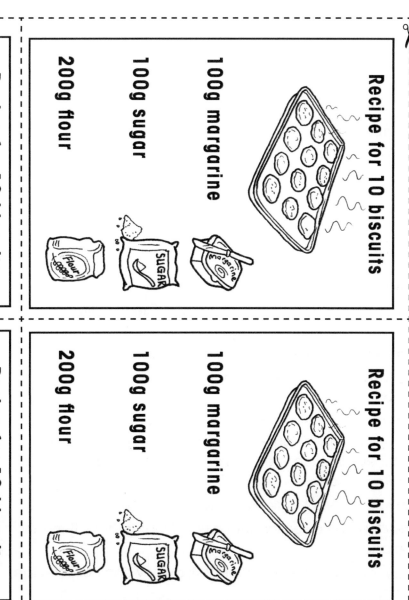

100g margarine

100g sugar

200g flour

Recipe for 10 biscuits

100g margarine

100g sugar

200g flour

Recipe for 10 biscuits

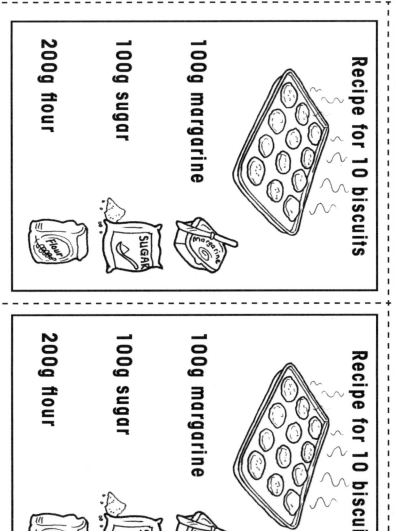

100g margarine

100g sugar

200g flour

Recipe for 10 biscuits

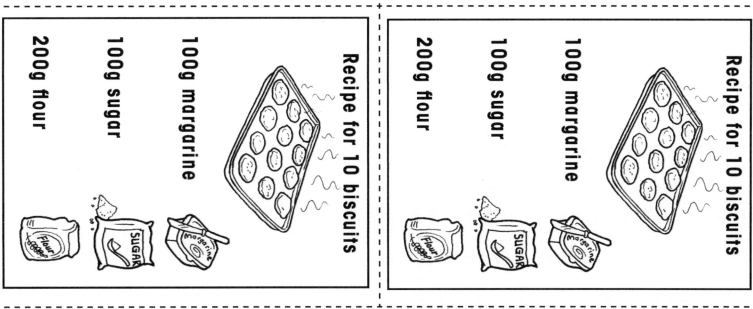

100g margarine

100g sugar

200g flour

Slide, slip and spill

Maths focus: developing understanding of 1 litre and $\frac{1}{2}$ litre and the link between them.

A game for two to four players

You will need:
- Game board (page 63).
- Coloured counter (or alternative) for each player.
- A 'Jug base board' for each player (page 64).
- A set of $\frac{1}{2}$ litre water strips (page 64).
- 1–6 dice (CD-ROM).

How to play

1. Players use the $\frac{1}{2}$ litre water strips to put 1 litre of water in their jugs.

2. Players then choose their starting positions.

3. Players take turns to roll the dice and move that number of spaces.

4. When they reach the outer track they can choose which way they go (clockwise or anti–clockwise). Once a player has chosen their direction, they can only travel that way round the track from now on.

5. Players take different actions depending on their roll:
   - If they land on a section with a water feature, they throw the dice again.
   - If they throw an even number (2, 4, 6) they can collect a litre of water.
   - If they throw an odd number (1, 3, 5) they can collect $\frac{1}{2}$ litre of water.

6. Players fill their jug using the $\frac{1}{2}$ litre water strips, starting at the bottom. They cannot have more than 3 litres, so if their jug is full they cannot take any more $\frac{1}{2}$ litre strips.

7. If they land on hazard spaces, they must follow the instructions. If a player has no water, and therefore cannot spill any, they go straight back to their start position and start their game again with 1 litre.

8. Play continues until all players are back at their 'START' position. The player with the most water in their jug is the winner.

Teaching notes
This game is designed so that players add to and take away from their original litre of water by using a combination of litres and $\frac{1}{2}$ litres. It uses their knowledge and understanding of the equivalence between two $\frac{1}{2}$ litres and 1 whole litre.

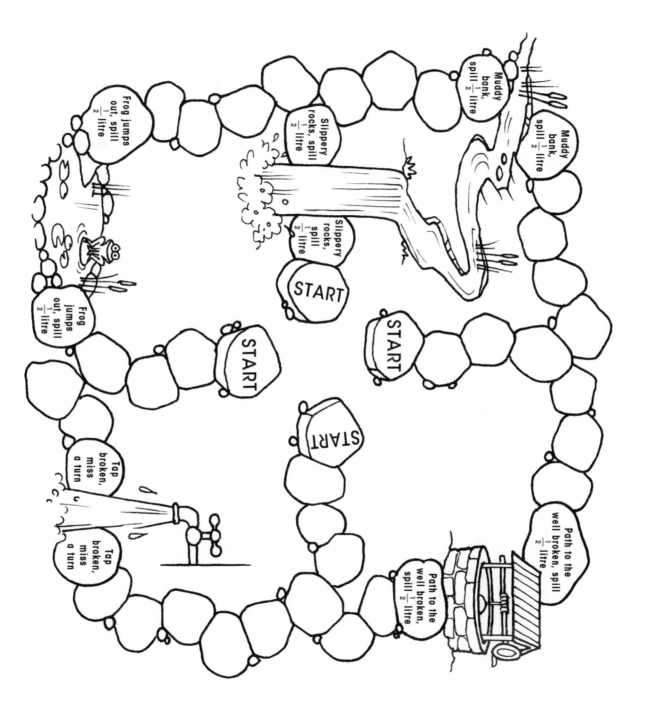

Slide, slip and spill – Jug base boards

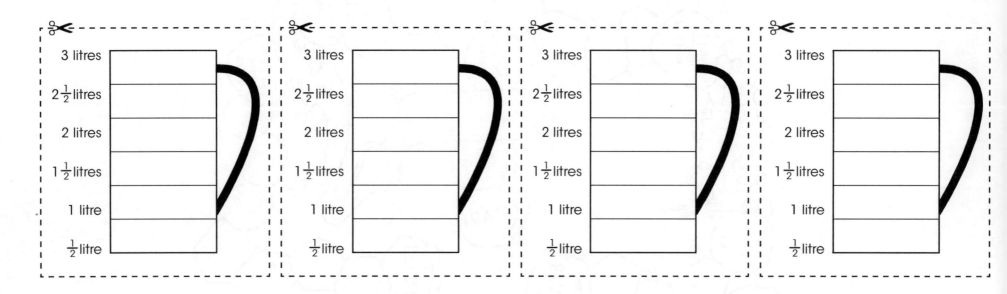

Slide, slip and spill – $\frac{1}{2}$ litre water strips

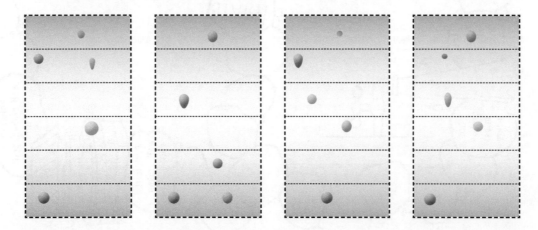

Hare and tortoise (1 and 2)

Maths focus: counting on correctly and timing accurately.

A game for two players

You will need:
- Game board (page 66).
- A playing piece each for each player (page 66).
- A 1–6 dice (CD-ROM).
- A stop watch.

How to play

Game 1

1. Players choose to be either the Hare or the Tortoise, then take turns to roll the dice:
   - If a 1, 2, 3 is thrown the Tortoise moves forwards that number of spaces.
   - If a 4, 5, 6 is thrown the Hare moves forwards that number of spaces.
   - If the Hare lands on carrots or lettuces, he misses a turn (while he eats the food).
   - If the Hare lands on a rain cloud he shelters from the rain for 10 seconds, and the tortoise can have as many turns as they can fit in during the 10 seconds. It is then the Hare's turn again and play continues as normal.
   - If the Hare lands on a butterfly he sleeps for 20 seconds, and the tortoise can have as many turns as they can fit in during the 20 seconds. It is then the Hare's turn again, and play continues as normal.

2. The player who reaches the 'FINISH' first is the winner. Will it be the Hare or the Tortoise? Play the game again. Did the same animal win?

Game 2

Ask players whether *Game 1* was a fair game. Challenge them to use the board, playing pieces, dice and stop watch to make a game of their own about a Hare and a Tortoise, then choose a partner to play it with them. Can they make the game better?

Teaching notes

This game is based on the Fable by Aesop called **The Tortoise and the Hare**. At the beginning of the game, the rules seem unfair because the Hare can move in larger jumps than the tortoise; giving the impression that the Hare will always win. However, the player who is the Hare might not roll a 4, 5, or 6 on each turn, and this player is also impacted by the obstacles. There are no obstacles or hazards for the tortoise. But the Hare may be lucky and miss them all.

Game 2 allows the players to discuss the game and look for a way to improve it. That could involve changing the rules, changing the times or changing the obstacles. It's up to the players!

Playing pieces – cut along the dashed line to separate the game board from the playing pieces.
Then cut out the pieces and give one to each player.

Hare and tortoise – Game board

Time travel (1 and 2)

Maths focus: calculating total amounts of time using knowledge of the relationships between consecutive units.

A game for two to four players

You will need:
- Game board (page 67).
- A counter (or alternative) per player.
- A 1–6 dice (CD-ROM).
- A set Game cards (page 68).
- Paper and pencil.

How to play
Shuffle the cards and place them face down on the board.

Game 1

1. Players 'START' on the earth and 'FINISH' on the moon.
2. Players take turns to roll the dice and move that number of spaces:
   - If a player lands on a star they take a card and keep it.
   - If a player lands on an instruction space they must follow the instruction.
3. When a player reaches the 'FINISH' (the moon) they calculate the times shown on their cards.
4. The player with the shortest amount of time is the winner, as they travelled to the moon the fastest.

Game 2

1. Play as for *Game 1*, but once at the moon the player must travel backwards along the board, to earth as the new finish, collecting time cards as they travel.
2. The winner is the player with the shortest amount of time once they get back to earth, as they took the shortest time to travel from the earth to the moon and back again.

Teaching notes
This game can be easily differentiated by:

1. The times used on the cards.
2. By the return or not to earth.

For less confident players: use whole totals of time to be added (hours, minutes, days).

For more confident players: parts of a minute, day, week or month can be used.

Use the time cards appropriate to the players.

Move back 3 spaces

Move on 3 spaces

Have another go

Miss a turn

Have another go

START

Time cards

Move back 3 spaces

Miss a turn

Move on 2 spaces

FINISH

Time travel – Game cards

15 seconds	30 seconds	45 seconds	60 seconds	10 seconds
1 minute	5 minutes	10 minutes	30 minutes	60 minutes
1 hour	5 hours	10 hours	15 hours	24 hours
1 day	2 days	4 days	6 days	7 days
1 week	2 weeks	3 weeks	4 weeks	1 month
3 months	5 months	8 months	12 months	1 year

Shape match (1-4)

Maths focus: recognising different shapes.

A game for two to three players

You will need:
- A set of Game cards (page 71).
- A set of blank cards (page 73).

How to play

Game 1

1. Shuffle the 2D shape cards together and then place the cards face down and spread out on a surface in front of the players.
2. Each player takes turns to turn over two cards, being careful to leave them in their current position for now.
3. If the two cards match, that player takes the cards. If they don't match, the cards are turned face down again and the other player has a turn.
4. When all of the cards have been taken, the player with the highest number of cards is the winner.

Game 2

1. Play as *Game 1* but add cards with the names of the shapes to the set of shape cards (use the set of blank cards).
2. If a player turns a shape card over and then the name of that shape, that counts as a matching pair, as do two cards showing the same shape, or two showing the same name.
3. Play continues as before with the player with most cards at the end being the winner.

Game 3

1. Play as *Game 2* but this time use the set of blank cards to write the properties of the shapes and add those to the other two sets.
2. In this game there will be six possible pairs for each shape: shape + shape; name + name; properties + properties; shape + name; shape + properties; name + properties.
3. Play continues until there are no more matching pairs.
4. The winner is the player with the most cards.

Game 4

1. As per *Game 3*. Using the blank cards, write other vocabulary to make matching cards, such as curved, straight, round, corner, point, face, side, edge.
2. These can be added to the other cards, or they can be used as a double set as their own game of matching.
3. Play continues as before.
4. The player with most cards at the end of the game is the winner.

Challenge

The shape cards contain 2D shapes and representations of 3D shapes. For a more challenging game, use both the 2D shape cards and the 3D shape cards and shuffle them together.
The blank cards can be used for the names and properties of the shapes, either 2D or 3D, as described above.

Shape match - 2D shape cards

Shape match – 3D shape cards

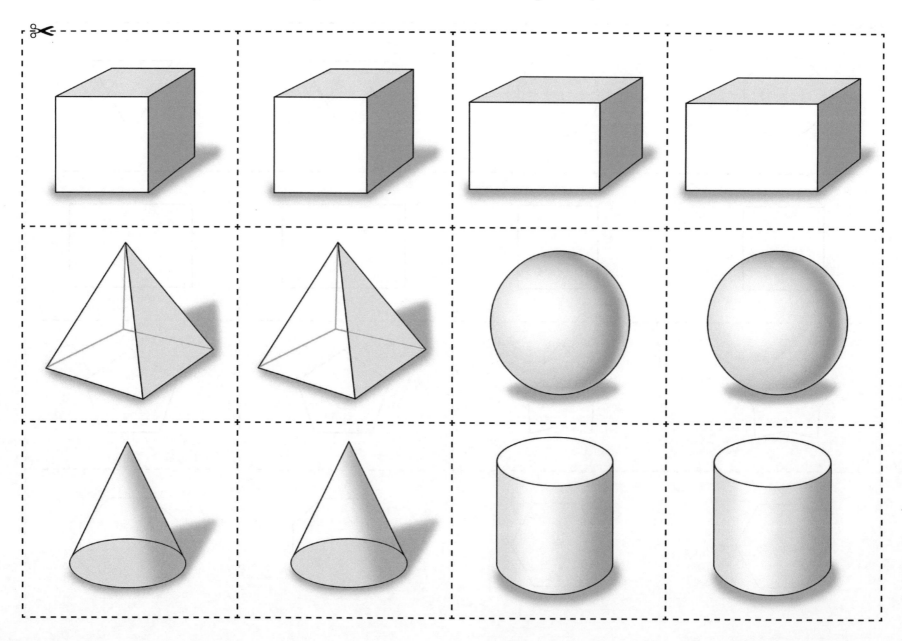

Shape match - Blank cards

Name that shape

Maths focus: naming and describing 3D shapes, referring to their properties.

A game for two players

You will need:
- Game board (page 75).
- Sets of 3D shapes (cubes, cuboids, cylinders, spheres, cones, pyramids).
- 1–4 spinner base (page 75).
- A counter (or alternative) for each player.
- A paper clip and pencil.

How to play

1. Player 1 places one end of the paper clip in the centre of the spinner base and holds it in place with the tip of a pencil, then flicks the paper clip so that it spins round and points to a number.
2. The player moves a counter that number of places along the track on the Game board.
3. The player looks at the 2D representation of the 3D shape they have landed on and chooses that shape from the set on the table.
4. The player names the shape and says two things they know about it. If they can do that, they keep the shape.
5. Play then passes to the next player.
6. Continue until both players have reached the 'FINISH'.

7. The winner is:
   - The player who can build the tallest tower with their shapes OR
   - The player who has the highest total of faces or edges OR
   - The player who can close their eyes, feel their shapes and can name them OR
   - The player who can ....You choose!

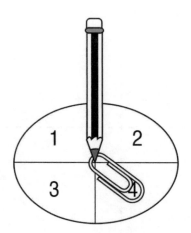

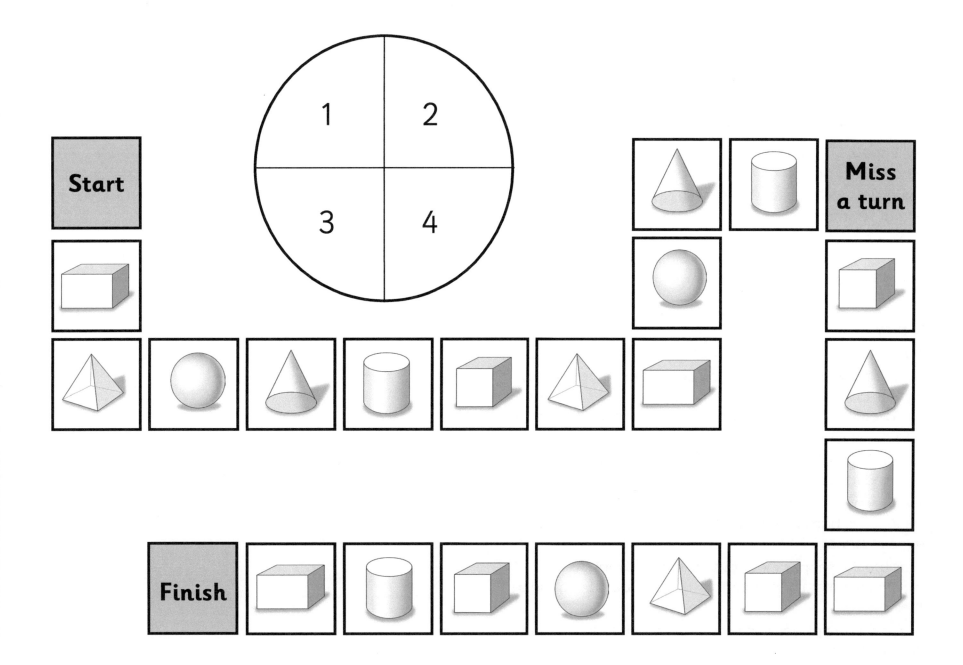

Collect and build shapes (1 and 2)

Maths focus: identifying reflective symmetry in patterns and 2D shapes.

A game for two to four players

You will need:
- Game board (page 77).
- A counter (or alternative) for each player.
- A line of symmetry for each player (paper or string).
- A 1–6 dice (CD-ROM).
- Set of shapes (different types of triangles, square, rectangle, four pointed star, pentagon, hexagon).

How to play

Game 1

1. Players start on any black hexagon on the Game board. They take turns to throw the dice and move that number of spaces in any direction. If they throw a 3, 4, 5 or 6 they collect a shape with that number of sides and say its name.

2. If they land on a pale grey hexagon they do not collect any shape and miss a turn.

3. When they have 12 shapes, they continue to throw the dice in order to move back to their start position but DO NOT collect any more shapes.

4. Players use the shapes they have collected to make a symmetrical pattern or picture. They may not be able to use all of their shapes.

5. The winner is the player who uses most of their shapes in their pattern or picture.

Game 2

Play as *Game 1* but the winner is declared differently. Players total the number of sides in their pattern (each triangle = 3, squares = 4). They take away the number of sides of any shapes they cannot use. The player with the highest total is the winner.

Teaching notes

Game 1 focuses on the collection, identification and use of shapes to make pictures or patterns with line symmetry. Players who are developing their understanding of this can use one line of symmetry, while other players can use two.

Game 2 also looks at and uses the properties of the shapes (number of sides) to calculate the value of the patterns made. You could also challenge the children to make their own shape/symmetry games which can be played in the classroom.

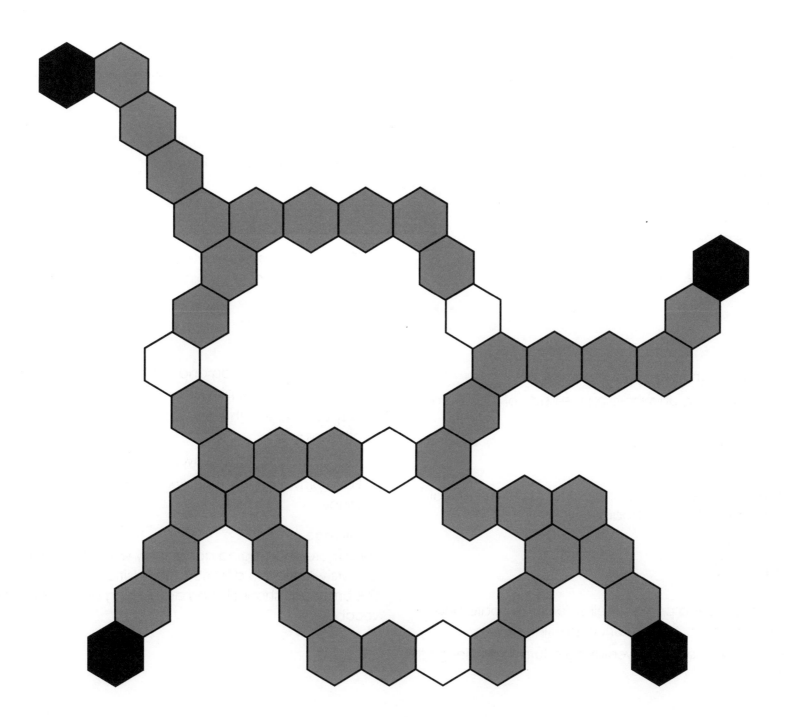

The symmetry game (1 and 2)

Maths focus: identifying reflective symmetry in patterns and 2D shapes.

A game for two players

> **You will need:**
> • One pegboard (also called pin boards or Geoboards).
> • Lines of symmetry (paper strips).
> • Pegs (or pins or elastic bands depending on the board).
> Other equipment such as building blocks or interlocking cubes can be used instead of pegboards.

How to play

Game 1

1. Place one line of symmetry on the pegboard.
2. Player 1 places a peg anywhere on their side of the board.

3. Player 2 places a peg of the same colour in a symmetrical position on their side of the board.

4. Player 2 then places a peg on their side of the board and Player 1 matches it in a symmetrical position.
5. Play continues with each player taking a turn to challenge the other player.

6. Play stops when one player cannot place a matching peg.
7. Each player counts their pegs. The player with most pegs is the winner.

Game 2

1. Place two perpendicular lines of symmetry on the pegboard.
2. Player 1 places a peg in one of the four sections.

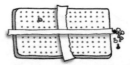

3. Player 2 places three more pegs of the same colour so that symmetry is shown across both lines.

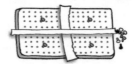

4. Player 2 places a peg and Player 1 matches it in the three other sections, keeping the symmetry across both lines.
5. Play continues with each player taking a turn to challenge the other player.
6. Play stops when one player cannot place matching pegs.
7. Each player counts their pegs. The player with most pegs is the winner.

Challenge

For a more challenging game, play with a barrier. In this case the players will need to describe the position of each peg they place. The emphasis should be on developing precise mathematical vocabulary.

Where is it?

Maths focus: recognising quarter turns as a right angle.

A game for two to four players

You will need:
- Game board (page 80).
- A set of Game cards (page 81).
- A 'player grid' for each player (page 82).
- A 1–6 dice (CD-ROM).
- Playing pieces (page 81).

How to play

1. Shuffle the destination cards and place them face down at the bottom of the board. Shuffle the direction cards and place them face down at the bottom of the board.

2. Each player takes one of the destination cards. That is the player's target destination. They travel to the destination by rolling the dice and using the direction cards.

3. Players begin on the 'START' square and place their playing piece so that the arrow points in the direction they are going/ facing. Player 1 rolls the dice and turns over a direction card, they then move that number of spaces in the direction indicated on the card, and it is the end of their turn. Each square counts as one, so rolling a 3 will move three squares. They can only move along the shaded (grey) squares.

4. If a player can't move in the direction selected (because they would fall off the grey path or off the grid) they miss a turn and use their next turn to select another direction card. If the next card presents an impossible direction, the player misses another turn and uses their next turn to select a new direction card. This continues until the player can move.

5. If a player reaches the edge of the grid before they have moved the amount they rolled, they have to stop. For example, if Player 1 rolled a 6 and after moving 4 reached the edge of the grid, they have to stop at the edge of the grid and end their turn. If a player reaches a junction ◄╬► before they have moved the amount they rolled, they can decide to end their turn there, or take a direction card. If they take a direction card, they have to move the remainder of their count in the new direction. For example, if Player 2 rolled a 6 and after moving 4 squares landed on the junction and decided to take a direction card, if the direction told them to turn 'a quarter-turn right' they would move the remaining two squares in the new direction.

6. To reach a destination, players must land on the 'star' square next to the artwork of the destination. When a player reaches their destination, they take another destination card and continue playing. If the destination card is the same as one they already had, it is returned to the bottom of the pile and the next card is chosen.

7. Play continues until a player wins by completing their 'player grid' with eight different destination cards.

This game uses a 2 × 4 'player grid', but change it to a 2 × 3 or 2 × 2 for some players if necessary.

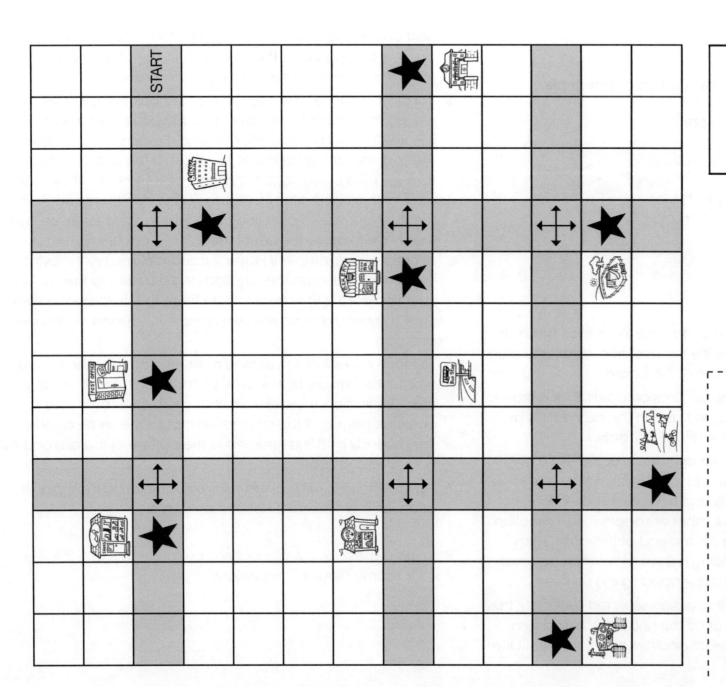

START

Direction cards

Direction cards

Cut along the dashed line to separate
the game board from the playing
pieces, then cut out each playing piece.

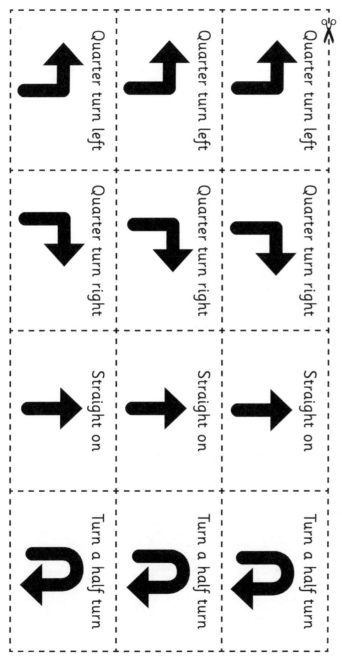

Where is it? – Direction cards

↰ Quarter turn left	↱ Quarter turn right
↰ Quarter turn left	↳ Quarter turn right
↰ Quarter turn left	↳ Quarter turn right
→ Straight on	→ Straight on
→ Straight on	
⮌ Turn a half turn	⮌ Turn a half turn
⮌ Turn a half turn	

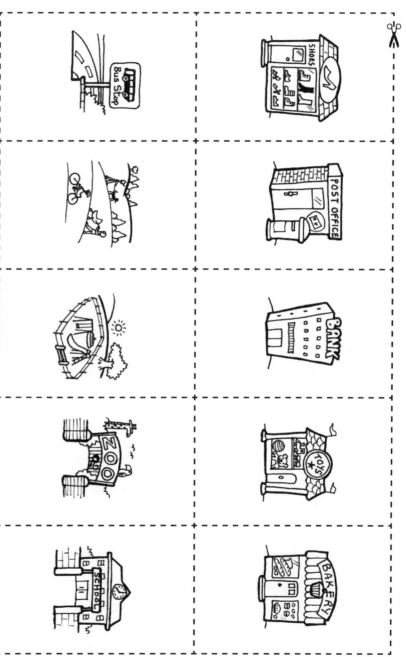

Where is it? – Destination cards

Track the Trolls (1 and 2)

Maths focus: practising constructing and interpreting a block graph.

A game for two to four players

You will need:
- Game board (page 84).
- A set of 'Who's the winner?' cards (page 87).
- A record sheet (page 85).
- A set of Game cards (page 86).
- A 1–6 dice (CD-ROM).

How to play

Game 1

1. Shuffle the 'Who's the winner?' cards and place them face down in the centre of the board. Each player picks one troll card from the game cards to be their playing piece that goes round the board. Each player must pick a troll with a different patterned T-shirt (spotty; vertical stripes; horizontal stripes/zig-zag).

2. Place the rest of the game cards on the table in piles according to T-shirt pattern.

3. Players take turns to throw the dice and move that number of spaces from 'START'.

4. If they land on a space with a troll they take a matching patterned troll card from the pile.

5. If they land on an instruction space, they follow the instruction.

6. Play continues until each player has reached the 'FINISH'.

7. Players then use the record sheet and the troll game they have collected to make a block graph.

8. When all the players have finished their graphs, turn over the top 'Who's the winner?' card from the centre of the board.

9. Read the card: And the winner is …

10. The player that fits the rule is the winner.

11. Place that card at the bottom of the pile if you want to play again.

Game 2

1. Play as for *Game 1*, but if players land on a troll which has the same pattern as their playing piece, they take a matching patterned troll card from the pile and also have another go.

Teaching notes

Both games are games of chance. The winner is not necessarily the player with most trolls, but is the player whose block graph matches the rule of the 'And the winner is …' card. This can be different each time the game is played. The players have to be able to construct their block graphs accurately, and be able to interpret/read them against the criteria on the 'Who is the winner?' card in order to determine who the winner is.

START

FINISH

Slip on ice. Move back 1 space.

Play in the snow. Miss a turn.

Make an ice slide. Move on 2 spaces.

Stop to watch the birds. Miss a turn.

Run to see a butterfly. Move on 2 spaces.

Chase a frog. Move back 2 spaces.

Swim in the river. Move on 2 spaces.

Stop to pick flowers. Miss a turn.

Collect your hat. Move back 2 spaces.

Play with leaves. Miss a turn.

Lose your way. Move back 2 spaces.

Join your friend. Move on 2 spaces.

And the winner is...

Track the trolls – Record sheets

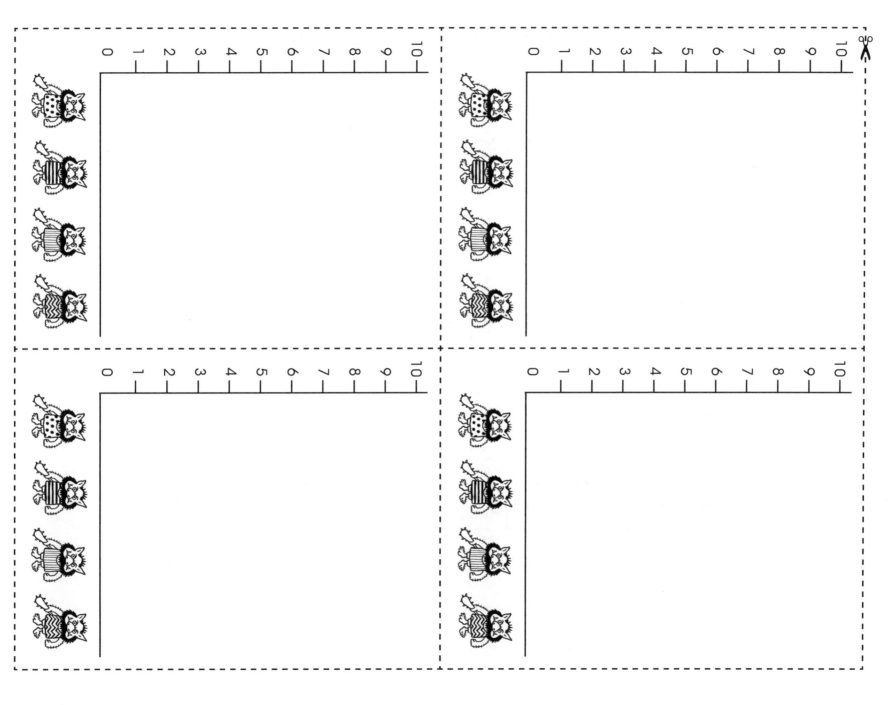

Track the trolls - Game cards

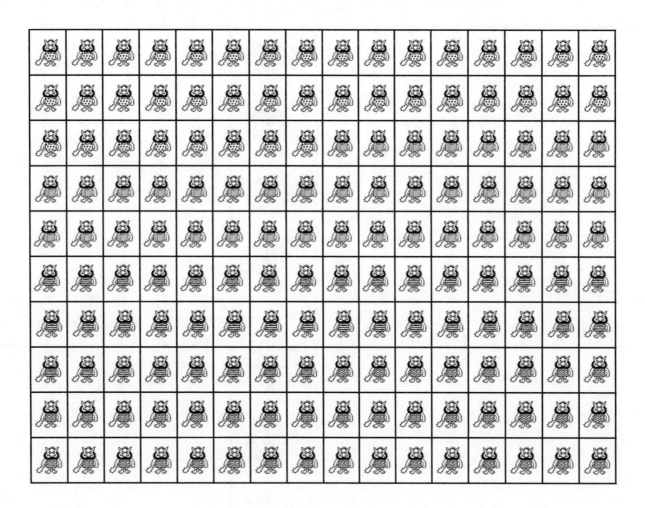

Track the trolls – 'Who's the winner?' cards

The player with the most spot trolls

The player with the most vertical stripe trolls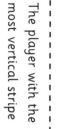

The player with the most spot and horizontal stripe trolls

The player with the most zigzag and horizontal stripe trolls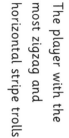

The player with the least spot trolls

The player with the least vertical stripe trolls

The player with the most spot and vertical stripe trolls

The player with the most vertical and horizontal stripe trolls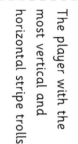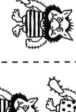

The player with the most horizontal stripe trolls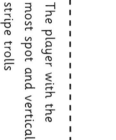

The player with the most zigzag trolls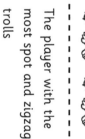

The player with the most spot and zigzag trolls

The player with the most trolls altogether

The player with the least horizontal stripe trolls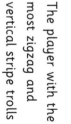

The player with the least zigzag trolls

The player with the most zigzag and vertical stripe trolls

The player with the least trolls altogether